Aberdeensh...
www.aberdee·
Renew·

4002704

Relics of the Reich

About the Author

Colin Philpott has a long-standing interest in recent German history and in abandoned buildings and venues.

His first book, 'A Place in History', looking at the impact on places where news stories happened in twentieth-century Britain, was published in 2012. His drama 'The Last Match', about the last day of peace before the Second World War, was first performed in 2014.

He is a former Director of the National Media Museum and was a BBC programme-maker and journalist for twenty-five years. Alongside his writing, he now works as a non-executive director, a producer on creative and media projects and as a radio and event presenter.

He lives in Yorkshire.

Relics of the Reich

The Buildings the Nazis Left Behind

Colin Philpott

Pen & Sword
MILITARY

First published in Great Britain in 2016 by
PEN AND SWORD MILITARY
an imprint of
Pen and Sword Books Ltd
47 Church Street
Barnsley
South Yorkshire S70 2AS

ISBN 978 1 47384 424 7

A CIP record for this book is available from the British Library.

Printed and bound in England by
CPI Group (UK) Ltd, Croydon, CR0 4YY

Typeset in Times by CHIC GRAPHICS

Pen & Sword Books Ltd incorporates the imprints of
Archaeology, Atlas, Aviation, Battleground, Discovery,
Family History, History, Maritime, Military, Naval, Politics,
Railways, Select, Social History, Transport, True Crime,
Claymore Press, Frontline Books, Leo Cooper, Praetorian Press,
Remember When, Seaforth Publishing and Wharncliffe.

For a complete list of Pen and Sword titles please contact
Pen and Sword Books Limited
47 Church Street, Barnsley, South Yorkshire, S70 2AS, England
E-mail: enquiries@pen-and-sword.co.uk
Website: www.pen-and-sword.co.uk

*This book is dedicated to
all the victims of National Socialism*

*   *   *

Contents

Introduction –
Collective Guilt?

(Kollektivschuld?)

Prora-Rügen Kraft durch Freude (Strength through Joy) Holiday Complex at Rügen Island on the Baltic Coast (George Wiora)

It was one of the darkest, albeit short-lived, periods in human history – the reign of terror unleashed by Nazi Germany in the 1930s and 1940s. The sense of shame, guilt and disgust associated with such an evil regime is heightened because it arose in an apparently developed, sophisticated and cultured country. After three quarters of a century an enduring fascination with the Third Reich remains even though very few people who could be said to be meaningfully complicit in its horror are still alive.

The Nazi story still exerts, particularly for people in the western democracies, a powerful hold. This is, of course, because of the industrial scale of the warmongering and genocide, the consequences of which still reverberate through history. It is also because of a need to understand whether the moral degradation to which Germany slumped was a particular product of a peculiar set of circumstances or whether it could have occurred elsewhere.

Inevitably, when studying the history of Nazi Germany, we are asking the question – how could this happen? How could a civilised nation allow itself to be taken in by such an evil philosophy? Much has been written and continues to be written about this but perhaps rather less attention has been given to an equally fascinating question – how did post-war Germany

The Holocaust Memorial was designed by Peter Eisenman and opened in 2004 on the sixtieth anniversary of the collapse of the Third Reich (Txalapartari)

recover from such a catastrophic episode in its history and rediscover the core values of civilised society, arguably as quickly as it had lost them?

The development of national rehabilitation for post-war Germans, both for those implicated in the Nazi era and the innocent generations who followed them, has involved coming to terms with the legacy of the Third Reich. This process is incomplete and still divides opinion. This book looks at one, hitherto relatively unexplored, aspect of this – the physical legacy of the Nazis, their buildings, their structures and their public spaces.

The Nazis were inveterate builders. Like many regimes, particularly dictatorships, one way they sought to secure their place in history and immortalise themselves and their ideas was through their architecture. They bequeathed a vast, largely unwanted, physical legacy to post-war Germany. Some of their buildings had been designed specifically as instruments of terror. Some were grandiose and built as statements. Some were functional and utilitarian. Hitler took a close personal interest in architecture and, aided by his loyal acolyte, the architect Albert Speer, built many and planned even more.

Seventy years after the Führer committed suicide in his Berlin bunker much of the architectural legacy left behind in 1945 remains with us. Nearly every member of the Nazi High Command died as the regime collapsed, either at their own hands or executed following the Nuremberg trials. It is, however, perhaps symbolic that Speer, who controversially escaped the noose at Nuremberg, survived (until 1981) and with him much of the architecture he created.

Immediately after the collapse of Nazi Germany in 1945 with the dislocation, disintegration and division that followed the fate of this architectural heritage was the least of Germany's worries. Some of the sites most symbolic of the evil of the regime were destroyed by the Allies. Many buildings were pressed into service with new uses as the desperate quest for survival took priority. Others remained ignored by a nation preoccupied with a harsh, daily grind and embarrassed by the physical detritus of the Third Reich. Furthermore the issue of the Nazi legacy, for several decades after 1945, became intertwined with the division of Germany and the playing out of the Cold War in that divided country.

Studying this physical legacy makes for a fascinating journey, not out of some morbid curiosity for a dark period of history, but because a sense of place, wanting to be there, and wanting to tread where history was made are undeniable parts of the human psyche. Focussing on the places where the deadly Nazi story unfolded serves to remind us of the depths to which humanity sank. It can also act as a commemoration of mankind's

The New Reich Chancellery with its grand interior designed by Albert Speer, Berlin, 1939 (Bundesarchiv, unknown)

Adolf Hitler and Eva Braun at the Führer's mountain retreat, the Berghof on the Obersalzberg in Bavaria, June 1942 (Bundesarchiv, unknown)

deliverance from a dark decade and serve as a renewal of our commitment to ensure history does not repeat itself.

This book examines a selection of places which feature in the Third Reich story. Most of them were built during the Nazi period although some predated it but were adopted by the Nazis. It is not a comprehensive list of every building and site associated with the Nazis nor is it some sort of 'dark tourism' travel guide. Where appropriate, the book contains my personal feelings about the experience of visiting these sites because doing so raises all sorts of questions about one's own motivations and reactions on seeing places so associated with such a terrible period.

The sites are organised chronologically as they fit into the story of the Nazis' rise and fall starting with places associated with their assumption of power; following through into their years in control of Germany in peacetime; touching on their creation of immense spaces (some built, others only remaining on the drawing board) designed to glorify National

Socialism; then moving into the war and the sites associated with their military machine; taking in the most chilling places of terror; and ending with the places associated with the regime's downfall. They feature both what the Germans call 'victim sites' and 'perpetrator sites'. Nearly all are in Germany itself although a few are outside. Many are now preserved, managed and publicly accessible.

Nothing in this book is meant to justify, celebrate or in any way explain away this most heinous of regimes. Rather, it is an attempt to tell the story, both individually and collectively, of the buildings the Nazis left behind and what has happened to the architecture of the Third Reich in the intervening years. This is a worthwhile story in its own right but, in chronicling this, it may also be possible to throw some light on the culture and soul of modern Germany as it has regained its place among the civilised nations of the world.

Colin Philpott
July 2015

The 'Arbeit macht frei' (Work sets you free) sign on the gates of the Dachau Concentration Camp (Dorsm365)

Chapter One

Establishing the Faith
(Gründung der Glaube)

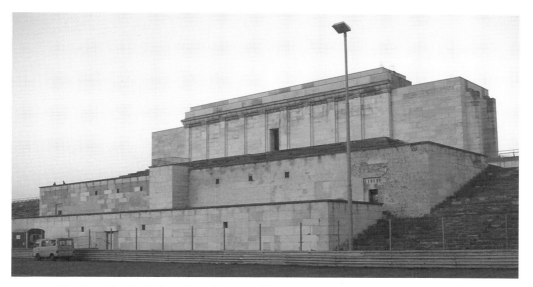

The Zeppelin Field Grandstand is one of the most iconic Nazi remains anywhere in Germany (Stephen Wagner)

PREAMBLE

Our first group of places associated with the Third Reich has one thing in common – all were either built, or appropriated by, the Nazis as symbolic locations designed to be part of the process of cementing the party's relationship with the German people. This was either done by providing great spaces where quasi-religious ceremonial would inculcate the philosophy of National Socialism by taking locations dating from earlier periods in German history and imbuing them with political significance or by investing an almost sacred aura to locations which were important in the early years of the Nazi movement. Most of these buildings are in Bavaria – the effective birthplace of the party – and associated mainly with the years before the Nazis came to power in 1933 or with the peacetime years of their rule before 1939.

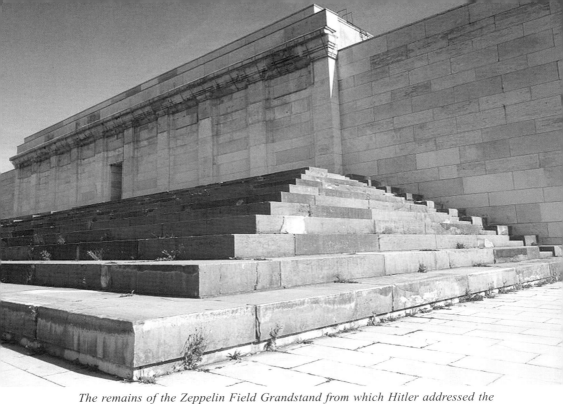

The remains of the Zeppelin Field Grandstand from which Hitler addressed the annual Nazi Party Rallies in Nuremberg (Adam Jones)

'Honouring the Fallen' on the Luitpoldarena, the original area used for the Nazi Party Rallies in Nuremberg, September 1934 (Bundesarchiv, unknown)

NUREMBERG RALLY GROUNDS, NUREMBERG, BAVARIA.

The tower blocks along the Beuthener Strasse on the south-eastern outskirts of Nuremberg symbolise the prosperity of twenty-first century Germany as a whole and Bavaria in particular. The road towards the city centre bears to the right unveiling the tell-tale shape of a much older structure; passing behind the building, even viewed from the back, the distinctive outline of one of the most recognisable structures of the Nazi era is clear. From the car park beyond the far end of the building emerges its full-frontal view already familiar through viewing newsreels and hundreds of still images.

The first time I set eyes upon the remains of the grandstand of the Zeppelin Field at the Nuremberg Rally Grounds some years ago I had that feeling that often happens when visiting somewhere iconic. It felt smaller than I imagined but, nevertheless, both chilling and awe-inspiring. Enough remains of the vast grandstand, where Hitler addressed the faithful throng gathered for the annual rallies, to get a sense of what it must have been like in the 1930s. More than seventy years on, aided by those newsreels, it is possible to imagine the searchlights, the music, the speeches and the serried ranks of disciples gathering for what was the biggest annual set piece of the Nazi calendar.

Nuremberg is a natural starting point for an examination of the buildings and spaces bequeathed to Germany by the Nazi regime. The Rally Grounds are one of the largest Nazi sites and arguably the most symbolic. It was probably the most important location in propaganda terms and the rallies held there played a major role in strengthening the hold of the Nazis over Germany, in developing the cult of personality around Hitler and in showing off Nazi Germany to the world. Along with a number of other places in the Nazis' birthplace of Bavaria, some built and others appropriated by them, it is part of the story of how they gained and maintained power.

The Zeppelin Field may be the image that comes most readily to mind when people think of the Nuremberg Rally Grounds but it was only one part of a vast area of south-eastern Nuremberg developed by the Nazis as their spiritual home. The city was chosen for two reasons – one symbolic and the other practical. Once the seat of the Imperial Diet of the Holy Roman Empire, seen by the Nazis as the First Reich, they believed there was a historical continuity in holding the rallies there. The practical reasons, however, were probably more important. Nuremberg was an important rail junction and a suitably central place for a gathering of large numbers of people from all over Germany.

The first Nazi Party rallies were held in Munich and Weimar but from 1927 onwards they took place in Nuremberg. Rallies were held there in 1927, 1929 and then from 1933 to 1938. The scheduled 1939 rally was cancelled at very short notice with the outbreak of war on 1 September. One

SA (Sturmabteilung) troops at the 1933 Nuremberg Rally – one of the eight held in the Bavarian city (Bundesarchiv, unknown)

The new Zeppelin field Grandstand, designed by Albert Speer to provide a bigger arena for the Nuremberg Rallies, 1934 (Nuremberg Rally Grounds Documentation Centre, unknown)

pre-existing building, the Luitpoldhalle, had originally been built for the Bavarian Exhibition in 1906 and was used for indoor meetings at the rallies but the other main public spaces and structures were designed and built by the Nazis – mainly by Hitler's architect, Albert Speer.

There were two main outdoor rally areas. The Luitpoldarena, used as the main arena for the 1927 and 1929 rallies, was a large open space which had previously been a park. Prior to the Nazis' seizure of power, the City of Nuremberg had built an Ehrenhalle or war memorial at one end of the park to commemorate German dead from the First World War. The Nazis converted the parkland into an open arena and built a grandstand at the far end of the park.

After the Nazi seizure of power in 1933, it was decided that the Luitpoldarena was inadequate to accommodate Hitler's growing ambition to stage even more grandiose spectacles. Speer was commissioned to build a new, larger arena on the neighbouring Zeppelin Field, so called because Ferdinand Graf von Zeppelin had landed one of his first airships there in 1909. The distinctive grandstand was around 350m wide and the arena could hold over 150,000 people.

There were, however, many other parts of the Nuremberg Rally Grounds built, or in many cases partially built, during the 1930s as Hitler and Speer let their megalomaniac ambitions have full reign during the pre-war years. Perhaps the most spectacular of all was the Congress Hall started in 1935 and planned as the party's national conference centre with an eye-watering capacity of 50,000 seats. Like many of the Nuremberg projects it remained unfinished. Likewise plans for a giant German Stadium, envisaged by Speer as the largest stadium in the world and capable of holding 400,000 people, were never fully realised. Construction began in 1938 but was halted with the outbreak of war (see Chapter Five). Similarly unfinished was the vision for the Marzfeld – a parade ground for the German Army envisaged to be the size of eighty football pitches.

There were three other main parts of the Rally Grounds complex. The KdF-Stadt (The Strength through Joy Village) was created to the north-east of the Rally Grounds housing accommodation for people attending the rallies as well as exhibition halls. An existing municipal stadium opened in 1928 was revamped as a venue for Hitler Youth events and sports activities. The Grosse Strasse (The Great Road) was built and completed to link the two ends of the grounds. It was almost 2km long and envisaged as a marching ground although never used for that purpose.

This agglomeration of buildings and public spaces became the focus each year for the Nuremberg Rallies whose objective was very simple. They were a propaganda exercise designed to demonstrate to the German people the strength and determination of the Nazi leadership and to show the world

Massed ranks of troops and supporters on the Zeppelin Field at Nuremberg during one of the Party Rallies which were the biggest annual set piece of the Nazi calendar (Bundesarchiv, unknown)

the unity of the German people under the Nazis. The rallies were full of ceremonial and sought to link Germany's past, present and future in quasi-religious symbolism but, in the speeches delivered there by the Nazi leadership often at great length, the raw militarism, racism and terror that were the hallmark of the regime were barely disguised. Leni Riefenstahl's famous film *'The Triumph of the Will'* captured the pageantry and theatre of the rallies which, despite their sinister intent, were a triumph of organisation and choreography.

The Nuremberg Rallies played a crucial role both internally and abroad in the development of pre-war Nazi power. Perhaps appropriately the story of what happened to this most iconic of Nazi sites after 1945 is a microcosm of what happened to the entire legacy of Nazi architecture after the collapse of the 'Thousand Year Reich'. Parts of the Rally Grounds were damaged by war and then demolished. Other parts were deliberately destroyed as part of the denazification process but many were put to new use and remain operative today.

For Nuremberg, though, the fate of the Rally Grounds was part of a much bigger challenge – how to deal with the city having become a toxic brand. Nuremberg was, in many ways, the heart of Nazism. It was there that the laws stripping Jews of their rights (the Nuremberg Laws) were first declared. It was, and still is, a city particularly associated with the Nazis and, mainly for that reason, it was the city chosen by the Allies to stage the post-war trials of the Nazi leaders. For more than fifty years before German reunification it struggled to deal appropriately with the unwanted physical legacy left in its midst by the Nazis.

At first, whilst the victorious Allies were an occupying force, it was they who took the decisions. In April 1945, before the war was over but after Nuremberg had fallen to the advancing Americans, the giant swastika on top of the Zeppelin Field grandstand was blown up. The Americans used the Zeppelin Field itself as a sports field and as a parade ground and the grandstand was used for concerts and other events. The American evangelist Billy Graham even preached there in 1963. After the grounds had reverted to the control of the City of Nuremberg the columns on the top tier of the grandstand were demolished for safety reasons and the area of the Zeppelin Field became a racetrack.

The Luitpoldhalle was severely damaged by Allied bombing in 1945, later demolished and is now a car park. The Luitpoldarena was returned to parkland in the 1950s – its Nazi grandstand there demolished but the Ehrenhalle war memorial remains. It would be quite possible to walk round this part of the grounds without realising its sinister history. Part of the grounds became a housing estate. A conference and trade fair centre were built elsewhere and the municipal stadium, refurbished several times, is the

The Ehrenhalle War Memorial, which predated the Nazis and which still remains, on the area of parkland which was the Luitpoldarena during the Third Reich (Magnus Gertkemper)

home of Nuremberg's football team and hosted several games in the 2006 World Cup. The Nuremberg Indoor Arena opened in the grounds in 2001.

The predominant approach to the redevelopment of the Rally Grounds site for at least twenty years after the end of the war was one of pragmatism. Paul B. Jaskot wrote in '*Beyond Berlin......Twelve German cities confront the Nazi Past*' that 'US Army and City officials treated the site as little more than a convenient set of bleachers'. For those unfamiliar with the term 'bleachers' are raised tiered rows of benches.

For many years after the war, there was a continuing reluctance to acknowledge the historical significance of the site. Nuremburg, as with much of the rest of Germany, had other preoccupations including rebuilding its city centre which had been flattened by Allied bombing towards the end of the war. As elsewhere in Germany in the immediate post-war period, its focus on survival contributed to seeing itself as a victim. It was, the narrative went, a victim of a war that had been lost, a victim of unjustified Allied bombing and it also saw itself as a victim of Nazism. Alongside this, of course, was the uncomfortable fact that many people in power in Nuremberg and elsewhere in Germany after 1945 had Nazi connections. The process of denazification, including prosecutions against former Nazis, slowed and effectively stopped in the 1950s and many former Nazis were assimilated back into public life.

Neil Gregor, in his study of the post-war history of the city, '*Haunted City; Nuremberg and the Nazi Past*', refers to how the citizens dealt with their own history in the 1950s and 1960s. At first they wrote of the city's history which, ignoring the Nazi period, harked back to Nuremberg's earlier medieval glory. By the 1960s the connection to the Nazi story was acknowledged but it was often presented as something that had been done to the city rather than with the active involvement of many citizens and certainly of its city council. Gregor writes that in this way the Nazis were represented as outsiders who came there 'for one week in a year to parade and hear speeches before departing again, leaving the ordinary citizens of Nuremberg to get on with their daily lives'.

From the 1960s, however, attitudes changed. A younger generation, learning about the Nazi period at school, started to question the silence of the older generations. As West Germany became economically buoyant and politically more self-confident the possibility of dealing with the difficult legacy of Nazism became real. In 1973 the Bavarian *Land (*Regional) Government classified the Rally Grounds as an historical monument. Only in the 1980s were specific ideas put forward for dealing with the parts of the grounds that were the most visible relics of the Nazi period – the Zeppelin Field grandstand and arena and the unfinished Congress Hall.

The first real acknowledgement of the historical significance of the site

The Reichsparteitagsgelände (Nazi Party Rally Grounds) Documentation Centre which opened in Nuremberg in 2001 in the remains of the Congress Hall building (Nuremberg Museums)

was the staging in 1985 of a temporary exhibition inside the mosaic hall of the Zeppelin Field grandstand entitled 'Fascination and Terror'. Later, after reunification, the debate about a permanent acknowledgement of the history of the site grew in intensity. It was caught up in changes of political control on the city council and also in the sometimes tortuous relationship between the city and the *Land* government of Bavaria. In 1999 the Federal Government agreed to help fund the project and in 2001 a museum-style Information Centre, or Documentation Centre as they are known in Germany, was opened describing the role that Nuremberg played in the Nazi story. Symbolically, a single shard of glass cutting through the building was incorporated into the design to demonstrate the break with the past. In 2006 interpretation boards were placed at various points around the site explaining its history.

235,000 people visited the centre in 2014 of whom forty per cent were from outside Germany. There are plans to extend the Documentation Centre including the building of a research centre. Elsewhere in the city the Palace of Justice, scene of the post-war Nuremberg trials of the Nazi leadership, is still in use as a court and a permanent exhibition there explains the story of the trials.

Hitler and Speer espoused the theory of 'ruin value' in their architecture. This was the idea, which Speer claimed incorrectly to have invented, that

Nuremberg must decide whether to spend 70 million Euros to preserve the remains of the Zeppelin Field (Mark Ahsmann)

buildings should be designed in such a way that they will leave behind aesthetically pleasing ruins when they eventually collapse. This was all part of a belief that Nazi architecture would speak to future generations and demonstrate the grandeur and importance of Nazi ideas hundreds of years later. In 2013, some eighty years after they were built, the structures of the Nuremberg Rally Grounds were in danger of collapsing. The City of Nuremberg estimated that around 70 million Euros might be needed to prevent collapse and make the structures safe.

An architectural study of the buildings was underway in 2015 and a decision is expected in 2016 on whether the project will go ahead. Politicians from most parties in Nuremberg seem to support the expense which will need financial support from both the Bavarian and Federal Governments. Opposition exists, however, and prominent among those expressing concern about the plans is the eminent German historian Norbert Frei who has argued that the buildings at Nuremberg should be allowed to crumble.

Nuremberg, meanwhile, has managed to return this area of the city in part to what it was before it was appropriated by the Nazis and it is once again a public open space – a 'lung' on the outskirts of the city. Whilst doing this, however, it has also acknowledged the historical significance of the site. As with iconic Nazi locations elsewhere in Germany it has, unsurprisingly, taken several generations for such reconciliation to be possible.

BÜRGERBRÄUKELLER AND THE HOFBRÄUHAUS, MUNICH, BAVARIA

Much of the early history of the Nazis in the 1920s involved beer halls – a slightly incongruous fact given Hitler's teetotalism. The two most famous

Munich beer halls in the Nazi story were the Bürgerbräukeller and the Hofbräuhaus.

The Hofbräuhaus is still in use. It was badly damaged by Allied bombing towards the end of the war but was repaired and reopened in the 1950s. Packed with locals and visitors, it is now part of the thriving tourist economy of Munich. Beer served in tall glasses is delivered to the tables in an exuberant fashion by waiters and waitresses in traditional Bavarian dress. While enjoying beer in the large main room it is difficult to connect the colourful vibrancy of twenty-first century Munich with the black and white images of Hitler and other Nazis delivering fiery speeches there almost a century ago.

The Hofbräuhaus dates back to 1589 and, by the beginning of the twentieth century, had become a major meeting place with a variety of function rooms as well as its main beer hall. It is said to have been frequented by Mozart and later by Lenin. It was well established as a venue for political meetings before the First World War and natural that the Nazis

Munich's premier beer hall, the Hofbräuhaus, is still a thriving tourist attraction but was the scene of many Nazi party meetings in the 1920s (Andrew Bossi)

Nazi party rally inside the Bürgerbräukeller, Munich, 1923 (Bundesarchiv, Heinrich Hoffman)

should use it. They are thought to have held their first meetings there in early 1920 – including on 24 February when Hitler delivered a twenty-five point National Socialist programme before 2,000 people. It is claimed that some of his earliest anti-Semitic speeches were delivered there. Unsurprisingly the account of the history of the Hofbräuhaus on its own website does not mention the Nazi connection.

The Bürgerbräukeller, which no longer exists, played an even more important role in the early Nazi story. Most famously it was the scene on 8 November 1923 of the so-called 'Beer Hall Putsch', Hitler's ultimately unsuccessful coup against the Bavarian government. The attempted putsch started with Hitler and other Nazi leaders storming a meeting of rival nationalist politicians taking place at the Bürgerbräukeller to try to force them to join in an uprising against the government. The attempted takeover soon turned into confusion and chaos but the following day a march by the Nazis through the city centre ended in a shoot-out with police. Sixteen Nazis and four policemen were killed. Hitler was arrested two days later, charged with treason and sent to prison for five years of which he only served nine months.

Thereafter, the 8 November held a special place in the Nazi calendar and each year the 'blood martyrs' of the failed putsch were commemorated with Hitler addressing the Nazi faithful in the Bürgerbräukeller. It was during one of these commemorations, in November 1939, that the second most famous connection between the building and the Nazi story took place. A bomb was placed in one of the pillars of the building and timed to explode during Hitler's address. It detonated killing eight people and injuring fifty-seven. Hitler, however, was not among them because, owing to bad weather, he had cut short his speech and left early to return to Berlin by train rather than by air.

Georg Elser was arrested in connection with the assassination attempt and held without trial for over five years. In early 1945 he was sent to Dachau concentration camp and was executed on Hitler's orders on 9 April. A number of conspiracy theories persist about the incident including the idea that the bombing was organised by the Nazis to create a sense that Hitler had been saved by divine providence. Most historians, however, believe that Elser acted alone.

The Bürgerbräukeller was severely damaged in the explosion and was never again used for the annual Beer Hall Putsch commemoration. After the war, it was used for a while as a club for American servicemen but was later reopened as a beer hall before being demolished in 1979. There is now no trace of it and a number of new buildings including a cultural centre and a hotel stand on the site. A nearby plaque commemorates Georg Elser's assassination attempt.

Both the Hofbräuhaus and the Bürgerbräukeller therefore enjoyed a special status in the Nazi party as key locations in the early 'years of struggle'.

WEWELSBURG CASTLE, PADERBORN, NORTH-RHINE WESTPHALIA

In the formative years of the party from the early 1920s onwards, the Nazis were keen to establish in the minds of the German people a philosophical basis for their policies. They were also quick to look for historical connections – ideas, historical figures and places – which linked them to earlier periods of German history.

As well as building arenas like the Nuremberg Rally Grounds where this inculcation could take place they also adopted a number of pre-existing buildings and spaces which they invested with a Nazi significance. The castle in the village of Wewelsburg near Paderborn in North-Rhine Westphalia was one of the most notorious of these.

Wewelsburg Castle was built in the early seventeenth century as a secondary residence for the Prince-Bishops of Paderborn. It was largely destroyed in the Thirty Years War, rebuilt, later damaged by fire and, in the

Wewelsburg Castle near Paderborn in North-Rhine Westphalia was a retreat for leaders of Heinrich Himmler's feared SS (Schutzstaffel) (Wewelsburg Kreismuseum)

Heinrich Himmler inside Wewelsburg Castle which he planned to turn into 'the centre of the world' as the headquarters of the SS (Unknown)

1920s owned by the local council. It was renovated as a youth hostel, museum, restaurant and banqueting hall.

After the Nazis came to power in 1933 Heinrich Himmler visited Wewelsburg and decided that its castle was a suitable location for an educational centre for the SS (Schutzstaffel or 'protection squad'). Work started on converting it and in September 1934 a ceremony was held to mark the opening of Wewelsburg Castle as an SS training centre. It was initially envisaged that the 'SS Schule Haus Wewelsburg' would provide education for the SS leadership but over the years its function appeared to change.

Himmler and other SS leaders were fascinated by the idea of studying German history in an attempt to bolster their theories of Aryan superiority. A range of research was conducted at Wewelsburg, including archaeological excavations, and Himmler had grand plans for further alterations to turn it into what he once grandly described as 'the centre of the world'. During the war Wewelsburg assumed a more prosaic function and was used as a meeting place for the SS leadership. Himmler also manifested a similar interest in Quedlinburg Castle in the Harz Mountains.

Heinrich Himmler at Quedlinburg Castle, another ancient location favoured by the Nazis (Unknown)

Interior of the Obergruppenführersaal at Wewelsburg Castle which can still be visited today (Sunnydog)

During the Third Reich, and since 1945, a whole series of rumours developed about Wewelsburg which has often been portrayed as a cult centre where SS leaders engaged in pagan ceremonies to buttress their ideology. The eerie nature of the place has contributed to this belief but those who now run the site museum doubt that such events ever took place.

In April 1945 Himmler ordered the destruction of Wewelsburg as the advancing Allied armies swept through Germany. It was restored soon after the war and reopened as a museum and a youth hostel in the 1950s. In the 1970s the site was designated as a war monument and an exhibition opened in 1982 detailing the story of the SS period in the castle's history. The exhibition was revamped in 2010. There is also a memorial at the nearby site of the Niederhagen Concentration Camp which supplied forced labour for the SS work at Wewelsburg. Part of the castle remains a youth hostel.

NEUE WACHE, BERLIN AND TANNENBERG MEMORIAL, POLAND

Two other examples of buildings which the Nazis 'adopted' for symbolic reasons were both war memorials – one in Berlin and the other in East Prussia, then in Germany but now in Poland.

The Neue Wache, Berlin which has been repurposed by different regimes several times during its 200 year history (Berlin Tourism Office)

Inside the Neue Wache on Berlin's Unter den Linden – during the Third Reich it was a major Nazi shrine (Daniel Schwein)

The Neue Wache, on the Unter den Linden in the heart of the German capital, had originally been built in 1816 as a guardhouse for the troops of the Crown Prince of Prussia. Its history over the past 200 years is a prime example of how a piece of architecture can be reinvented to serve different political ideologies in different eras.

By the end of the nineteenth century its function had become purely ceremonial and it was one of a number of buildings in Berlin demonstrating Prussian power and confidence. By the end of the First World War it had fallen into disrepair and, under the Weimar Republic in 1931, it became a war memorial officially approved by the Prussian State Government to commemorate the victims of the Great War.

Just two years later, after assuming power, the Nazis had their own view of how to utilize this grand building situated on Germany's grandest street for their political purposes. Previously Germany had commemorated its war dead with an annual remembrance day but the Nazis changed its emphasis and renamed it Heldengedenktag, the Day of Commemoration of Heroes. Between 1934 and 1945 the day was celebrated and the Neue Wache became the focus of the commemoration in the Reich capital. The annual

Crowds gathering at the Neue Wache, for the Annual 'Day of Commemoration of Heroes', 1938 (Bundesarchiv, A.Frankel)

'A Mother with her Dead Son' by the German sculptor Käthe Kollwitz, inside the Neue Wache after it was rededicated following German reunification (Berlin Tourism Office).

event concentrated on celebrating military heroes rather than the remembrance of the fallen. It was heavily damaged during the Battle of Berlin at the end of the war.

After the division of Germany the Neue Wache came within the Soviet zone in Berlin and, in 1960, the East German authorities restored and reopened it as a 'Memorial to the Victims of Fascism and Militarism'. After reunification it underwent a further reinvention and was rededicated in 1993 as the 'Central Memorial of the Federal Republic of Germany to the victims of war and dictatorship'. At the suggestion of the then German Chancellor, Helmut Kohl, the sculptures which had been placed inside the Neue Wache during the German Democratic Republic (GDR) era were removed. They were replaced by a sculpture originally made in 1937 entitled 'A Mother with her Dead Son' by the eminent German sculptor, Käthe Kollwitz.

The Tannenberg Memorial, in what is now Poland, is an even clearer example of the Nazi appropriation of a building to suit their political purposes. The vast memorial was built in 1924 near the town of Hohenstein in East Prussia to commemorate the nearby 1914 Battle of Tannenberg. It was octagonal in shape with eight, 20m high towers. The memorial was dedicated on the tenth anniversary of the battle by its hero, Paul von Hindenburg, who later became the German President and who eventually asked Hitler to form a government in 1933.

Hindenburg's death in August 1934 provided the Nazis with an opportunity to turn his funeral into a major propaganda event. His coffin

The rededication of the graves of former President Paul von Hindenburg and his wife at a ceremony at the Tannenberg Memorial, 1935 in what was then East Prussia (Bundesarchiv, Unknown)

was transported to the memorial and he was buried under the central plaza but, a year later, he and his wife were moved to a new chamber under the south tower with a further ceremony. Thereafter Tannenberg was portrayed as a place of national pilgrimage.

A decade later this shrine to German military honour had become a virtual ruin. In January 1945, with the Russians advancing from the east, Hitler ordered the disinterment of the Hindenburg coffins and their removal to safety further west. These were subsequently discovered by American troops and reburied in a church in Marburg where they remain. Much of the memorial was blown up by the retreating Germans in early 1945.

In 1949, with the area under Polish control, the Government in Warsaw ordered the dismantling of the remaining ruins of the memorial – a process which continued for several decades. Some of the remains have found their way to other places. The lion sculpture which once adorned the entrance is now displayed in a square in the nearby town of Olsztynek. Some of the granite from the memorial was used to build war memorials and a Communist party building in Warsaw. Today little remains to indicate that such a giant structure ever stood there.

There is, however, a curious footnote to the story of the Tannenberg

The Tannenberg Memorial from the air in 1944 not long before the Nazis ordered its destruction ahead of the Russian advance into East Prussia (Bundesarchiv, Siertstorpff)

There is very little evidence left of the Tannenberg Memorial on the site where it once stood near the town of what is now Olsztynek in Poland (Unknown)

The replica of the Tannenberg Memorial built at Oberschleissheim, near Munich to commemorate the Germans expelled from East Prussia after the Second World War (Tannenberg Denkmal)

Memorial to be found a long way from the site of the original. A much smaller replica of the memorial was dedicated at Oberschleissheim near Munich in 1984. It was a fifth of the size of the original with a 7m high oak cross in the centre. Created to commemorate the Germans who were expelled from East Prussia after the Second World War it was vandalised in 2008. The site is now used as meeting place by the Centre for German-Polish Youth Exchange.

BROWN HOUSE AND EHRENTEMPEL MUNICH, BAVARIA

At the end of April 2015, a new Nazi Documentation Centre opened in Munich detailing the story of the city's role in the Nazi era. The opening, on the seventieth anniversary of the end of the Nazi regime, was a highly significant event in the continuing debate over Germany's handling of the Third Reich legacy. Politicians, academics, families of victims and citizens of the Bavarian capital had argued for decades about the need for such a centre and, if so, what form it should take. The view from elsewhere in Germany and from many inside Munich was that the city, often dubbed 'The Capital of the Movement', had been too slow to acknowledge its complicity and significance in the emergence of Hitler and his party.

The Documentation Centre was opened on the site of one of the most important buildings bequeathed by the Nazis to Munich – the Braunes Haus, or Brown House, on Brienner Strasse. The building, which was originally built in 1828 as a private residence called the Barlow Palace, was offered by its owner to the Nazi Party. It was agreed that the gifted building should replace the party's existing undersized national headquarters in the city and conversion work was undertaken prior to the opening on 1 January 1931. Hitler and a number of other leading Nazis maintained offices there.

The Brown House, named after the brown shirts of the SA (Sturmabteilung) or Storm Detachment, suffered bomb damage in 1943 and was then largely destroyed in further raids towards the end of the war. The rubble was cleared away shortly after the war and the area remained empty until it was identified as the site for the new Documentation Centre. The choice of the site was partly pragmatic. It was an available piece of land owned by the Bavarian Government but was, of course, also a highly symbolic location as the former site of the Nazi movement's national headquarters.

The Brown House was only one of a number of buildings in a small area of Munich just north of the city centre which became the hub of the Nazi Party administration centred around, or close to, the Königsplatz. This square, originally laid out in the nineteenth-century for Crown Prince Ludwig of Bavaria, is another example of a space appropriated by the Nazis.

The new Nazi Documentation Centre opened in April 2015 in Munich on the site of the former Braunes Haus, once the Nazi Party HQ (Munich Tourism Office)

Braunes Haus, Munich, 1935 – one of a number of buildings which formed the administrative centre of the Nazi Party in Munich (Bundesarchiv, unknown)

Nazi ceremonial at the Ehrentempel in the Königsplatz in 1936 honouring the Munich Beer Hall Putsch 'martyrs' (Bundesarchiv, unknown)

Its grand dimensions and neo-classical style appealed to Hitler as an area for rallies and ceremonial. Three sides of the square were occupied by existing buildings. He replaced the lawns of the square with granite and a number of new buildings were erected around or near the square.

Most symbolic were the Ehrentempel, two mausoleums built in 1935 on the eastern side of the square, as the resting places for the sixteen Nazis killed in the 1923 Beer Hall Putsch. The Ehrentempel were dedicated with great pomp with eight of the so-called martyrs entombed in each of the two temples. Two imposing office buildings were also constructed near the square – the Führerbau and the Administration building – both on Arcisstrasse. Hitler used the Führerbau (which later acquired a particular historical significance – see Chapter Four) for entertaining when in Munich and the Administration building, along with the Brown House, was the headquarters of the party bureaucracy.

Both the Führerbau and the Administration building remain but the Ehrentempel have disappeared. In 1945 the Americans removed the bodies, contacted the families and had the men buried elsewhere. The structures

The Königsplatz area of Munich, the Nazi heart of the city including the Ehrentempel, Munich, 1937 (Bundesarchiv, unknown)

were dismantled and the materials recycled for other uses. Two years later the columns were blown up and trees and bushes have since overgrown the site although some of the original stonework is still visible. The Königsplatz became a carpark after the war but, in the 1980s, it was returned to its pre-Nazi layout with lawns.

Behind these bald facts lies a complicated and protracted debate about how Munich has handled its Nazi past. Only in the 1980s did an open debate start about how to deal with this difficult part of the city's legacy. Munich has subsequently taken longer than other cities to acknowledge its role in the development of National Socialism.

It is perhaps understandable that Munich should have found it a much more sensitive subject than some other cities whose role in, and connection with, the Third Reich, was weaker. As Gavriel D.Rosenfeld says in his study of Munich, *'Beyond Berlin…Twelve German Cities confront the Nazi Past'*, 'Munich arguably had most difficulty in coming to terms with its Nazi legacy because it had been "Capital of the Movement".' Moreover, the debates about the Nazi legacy became intertwined in political differences between the two main parties, the left of centre SPD and the conservative CSU, and also in differences of view between the city council and the Bavarian *Land* government – owner of the site of the proposed centre having inherited Nazi party property after 1945. The generally CSU-led Bavarian government was less in favour of establishing the centre than the generally SPD-controlled City Council.

The practical upshot of all this was twofold. For many years there was relative inaction although a number of buildings connected with the Nazis were demolished partly because of that association and partly for other reasons. During the late 1960s and early 1970s Munich was focussed on showing itself as a modern city deserving its role as host of the 1972 Olympic Games – another reason for ignoring the Nazi relics.

The idea of a Documentation Centre detailing Munich's role in the Nazi story was first discussed openly in the 1980s but it wasn't until 2002 that the Bavarian Parliament approved the idea in agreement with the City of Munich. Many commentators observed that Munich was shamed into action by other cities, including Nuremberg and Berlin, which had already started down this journey.

That decision was not, however, the end of the story and another thirteen years elapsed before the Centre opened. During this time there were differing opinions on what the Centre should be, or even if it should be a single building or a series of interpretation boards around the city. Views also differed as to whether the Centre should try to tell a comprehensive story about the Nazis or merely concentrate on Munich's role.

Hitler with supporters inside the Braunes Haus, Munich in the 1920s – Munich was seen as 'Capital of the Movement' (Bundesarchiv, unknown)

There is very little trace left of the Ehrentempel in Arcisstrasse, Munich (David Holt)

In the end the Centre that opened on the anniversary of the American liberation of Munich opted to be largely the latter and it follows the style of similar centres elsewhere. It contains permanent and temporary exhibitions, a research centre and an accompanying learning programme. The permanent exhibition covers four floors telling four different aspects of Munich's role in the Nazi story – the rise to power, the pre-war era, wartime, and the city's post-war treatment of its legacy.

The Centre has cost twenty-eight million Euros funded jointly by the City, *Land* and Federal governments. The running costs are being met by the City and there is an admission charge for adults. The Centre is hoping to attract up to 250,000 visitors a year.

SUMMARY
Studying this first group of Nazi sites reveals a number of themes. Firstly, the different approaches and differing speeds with which two Bavarian cities, Munich and Nuremberg, have tackled the Third Reich's legacy. Both cities have an inextricable link with the Nazis – Nuremberg arguably even more than Munich from an international perspective. Both took a long time to acknowledge the historical significance of the buildings and spaces left from the Nazi period but Nuremberg did so more quickly. It is easy to ascribe this to a host of political factors including the guilt associated with

Munich's position as 'Capital of the Movement' but there were also some very practical considerations. Nuremberg had to do something with the Rally Grounds – a vast area with buildings given historical monument status. In addition, there was an existing building, the Congress Hall, able to house the Documentation Centre. In Munich a new structure was required to achieve a Documentation Centre and this, perhaps, also made it easier to ignore the part of the city most associated with the Nazis.

The second main theme is that sites which the Nazis appropriated have, by and large, been returned to their pre-Third Reich use. So Wewelsburg Castle, the Neue Wache and the Hofbräuhaus are once again in use for the purposes they fulfilled before National Socialism. That is even true of the Nuremberg Rally Grounds which were a public area including parkland and a sports stadium before appropriation by the Nazis.

The third theme to emerge is one that will run through this story – one of pragmatism. Even some of the buildings constructed by the Nazis, like the Nazi Administration building in Munich, have been retained and put to new use. It is now an exhibition space for art shows. The idea that every Nazi construction is somehow tainted by association has not been accepted by most German cities and examples of the reuse of such buildings can be found almost everywhere.

Chapter Two

Strength Through Joy
(Kraft Durch Freude)

PREAMBLE

Not only did the Nazis seek to strengthen their hold over Germany through the vast propaganda machine embodied in events like the Nuremberg Rallies but they also used the power of the state to provide a whole range of material improvements to everyday life. It was a variety of 'carrot and stick' approach – propaganda and terror (more of that later) but also, as the regime saw it, improving the life of its citizens. This, of course, also boosted the economy and embedded the regime in popular affection.

Much of this was delivered by the vast KdF (Kraft durch Freude) or "Strength through Joy" organisation, part of the German Labour Front. It

Construction of what was said to be the biggest holiday complex in the world on the Baltic coast, the Prora-Rügen KdF (Strength through Joy) complex, 1937 (Bundesarchiv, unknown)

organised sporting and leisure activities in the workplace and elsewhere as well as holidays including cruises. It was said to be the world's largest tourism operator in the 1930s and its most ambitious project was a holiday camp on the Baltic coast – thought to be the world's biggest.

In addition, the Nazi regime also built many other structures designed to demonstrate that National Socialism was creating a modern, consumer society which would become the envy of the world. The Nazis didn't invent the idea of the motorway but they adopted it and developed it at a furious pace once they were in power.

Another aspect was the provision of spaces for Nazi-approved culture. Amongst locations of this type were the 'Haus der Deutschen Kunst', the House of German Art, an art gallery in Munich designed to show off 'pure German art'. They also constructed a series of outdoor amphitheatres or 'Thingstätten' across Germany as auditoria for concerts, plays and other cultural events.

Alongside these Nazi expressions of public and communal nation-building, the regime leaders were also quick off the mark to ensure that they were able to relish life's comforts. They soon enjoyed an opulent standard of living and built, or in some cases appropriated, grand private dwellings – many of them in the Bavarian mountains.

The post-war fate of these groups of buildings, both public and private, offers more evidence of the challenges faced by modern Germany in dealing with its Nazi heritage.

PRORA-RÜGEN KdF HOLIDAY COMPLEX, RÜGEN ISLAND, MECKLENBURG-WESTERN POMERANIA

The Nuremberg Rally Grounds are the most iconic surviving Nazi site and, arguably, the Prora-Rügen holiday complex on the Baltic coast is the most surreal. Its post-war fate also symbolizes the continuing debates about what to do with Third Reich buildings.

Prora-Rügen was conceived as a giant 'Strength through Joy' holiday camp which would provide seaside holidays for the German masses on the Baltic coastline. It was designed to accommodate 20,000 holidaymakers in eight huge buildings which extended almost 5km along the beach. The complex was designed following an architectural competition overseen by Albert Speer and, as well as the eight housing blocks, there were plans for swimming pools, theatres, cinemas and a festival hall which could have accommodated all 20,000 people staying there at one time.

Construction of the complex started in 1936 but was stopped on the outbreak of war in 1939. It was never completed and no one ever had a holiday there under the Nazis. During the war some Hamburg residents, escaping the Allied bombing of their city, took refuge in one of the blocks.

The remains of one of the blocks at the KdF Prora-Rügen complex dominate this part of the North German coastline (unknown)

Work on the Prora-Rügen holiday complex was never completed as it was abandoned on the outbreak of the war in 1939 (unknown)

The complex became part of the Soviet occupation zone after 1945 and some of the buildings were turned over to military use. A Soviet artillery brigade occupied one of the eight blocks. Many of the others were stripped of their useful materials and two of the eight blocks were demolished in the late 1940s.

After its handover to the East German authorities in the 1950s Prora remained a military facility. It was used by the National People's Army of the GDR as a training area and public access was restricted. Part of the complex was also used as an army convalescent home.

Prora retained its military use after German reunification in 1990 with the army of the united Germany, the Bundeswehr, taking control of it and using it for a while as a technical school. There was much discussion in the 1990s about demolition of the blocks but instead they were given historic monument status. Thereafter, for the first time since 1945, there was some acknowledgement of the historical significance of the site. Controversy has continued to dog plans for its future.

Temporary exhibitions and then a more permanent museum, or Documentation Centre, about Prora KdF were established in one of the blocks. More recently a separate museum detailing the site's role during the GDR era was also opened. On average around 80,000 visitors a year come to the Prora KdF museum which relies on entry charges to survive.

Promotional image of some of the new holiday apartments being created at Prora-Rügen (Standpark)

Of the six remaining blocks, one is in ruins. But four of the five surviving structures have been acquired by private investors who are at various stages of converting the blocks into holiday apartments, a hotel and other facilities. The fifth surviving block contains a new youth hostel opened in 2011 with 400 beds and funded by the local and federal governments. After seventy-five years something similar to the original purpose of the Prora complex is, thus, being realised.

Local opinion has been divided about these developments. For some it is a sensible use of buildings which are now legally protected and better being put to productive use than left to rot. Others regard them as irredeemably ugly, forever tainted by their Nazi provenance, and believe that they should be torn down. It is wrong, they argue, for money to be made by developers who, it is suggested, are realising Hitler's three-quarters of a century old dream. There is, however, a suspicion that some of the opposition to the redevelopment has come from nearby holiday resorts worried about the competition that the luxury seaside accommodation will provide.

Prora-Rügen encapsulates many of the dilemmas surrounding the Nazi architectural legacy in modern Germany. On the one hand these outsized buildings are arguably seriously out of place and out of scale with their surroundings; even compared with the worst examples on Europe's Mediterranean coastline they must rank as some of the ugliest holiday accommodation ever built. Their ugliness is, in part, an ugliness of association. Being the monumental product of an evil regime it can be very difficult to look at them other than as sinister.

It might also be difficult to imagine a complex of such scale being built in other countries in the 1930s but the style of architecture is not without parallel elsewhere. On the other hand like many other Nazi buildings, and apart from those specifically designed as places of terror, their purpose was not of itself sinister. It is this which has allowed many to see buildings like Prora in a very different light to concentration camps and even the Rally Grounds at Nuremberg.

Since work stopped on building the original Prora resort decisions about what to do with these vast edifices bequeathed from the Nazi period have been largely pragmatic. First, the buildings were put to military use and now, with the passage of time, there is a sense that their association with the Nazi era should not prevent them being regenerated even for their original purpose as a holiday destination.

As the redevelopment progresses it is by no means certain that the acknowledgement of the historical significance of the site will continue. The future of both Prora Museums is not guaranteed and currently the owner of the block where they are situated is allowing them to continue only on a year by year agreement.

No one ever had a holiday at the Prora-Rügen KdF holiday complex during the Third Reich but the buildings remain (unknown)

GERMAN AUTOBAHN NETWORK

Two of the most persistent myths about 1930s European fascism are that Mussolini made Italian trains run on time and that Hitler invented the idea of the *autobahn*, or motorway. The Nazis saw political and economic value in developing a motorway network across Germany and put considerable effort into motorway building after they came to power but they did not invent the idea and there were a number of precursors of the autobahn network.

The first was a private section of road, about 10km long, built near Berlin just before the First World War. It was the idea of a group of car enthusiasts who wanted to create a 'car-only road'. In fact it was mainly used for testing cars and for motor sport. In 1926 an association had been formed to lobby for the idea of a motorway linking Hamburg, Frankfurt and Basel in Switzerland, the so-called "HaFraBa" initiative. Much planning had been done although no construction had started. In August 1932, five months before the Nazis came to power, a section of public motorway was opened between Cologne and Bonn. It was financed by the City of Cologne and opened by its Mayor, Konrad Adenauer, who was to become the first post-war Chancellor of West Germany. There were also a series of plans in various stages of preparation for motorway style roads in several other parts of Germany although none had got off the drawing board.

Part of the new German autobahn network in the late 1930s – Hitler, Speer and Todt were interested in the aesthetics of motorways as well as their practical benefits (US Library of Congress)

Prior to 1933, the Nazis had been lukewarm about the idea of motorways but, once in power, Hitler saw their propaganda and economic value. The notion of creating mobility across Germany for ordinary people through a modern motorway network and the production of affordable cars appealed to the Führer. Within days of coming into office, Hitler appointed his chief engineer, Fritz Todt, to design and begin a programme of 'Reichsautobahn' construction with a target of 1,000km of new roads each year.

In September 1933 Hitler marked the beginning of the Nazi programme of road building by shovelling dirt in a ceremony on the banks of the Main in Frankfurt – one of a number of motorway construction sites across Germany. The first section built under the Nazis was opened, amid great propaganda fanfare, between Frankfurt and Darmstadt in May 1935. Construction of motorways across Germany continued up to the early years of the war and by 1939 almost 4,000km had been completed. At the time, although much less than the original targets, this was one of the most extensive motorway networks built anywhere in the world.

Like almost everything about the Nazis there was a dark side to this investment in infrastructure. Working conditions for labourers were, by all accounts, grim and autobahn construction workers who went on strike often found themselves hauled away for interrogation. By the latter part of the 1930s the shortage of labour for the motorway programme necessitated forced labour and, during the war, forced labour from concentration camps.

The idea that the building of the motorway network was a key element in achieving full employment in Nazi Germany is questionable. Originally there had been exaggerated claims that the road building programme would create as many as 600,000 jobs but the true number was much lower – probably around 120,000. Full employment in the Third Reich only arrived once the massive rearmament programme began in the mid-1930s.

Another widely held notion about the Nazis' affection for motorway building is that their real motive was military. The idea that they were primarily interested in creating the network for transporting people and materials in war is probably wrong. After the outbreak of war very little military use was made of the autobahn network as rail transport was seen as more useful.

Hitler digging foundations of one of the first sections of autobahn built after the Nazis came to power near Frankfurt, 1933 (Bundesarchiv, Unknown)

Todt, Speer and Hitler were interested in the aesthetics and saw the symbolism of motorways snaking across the Fatherland as something that unified the Reich. The standard design of the network, the rules about curves and intersections, were all part of creating an aesthetic that spoke to their vision of the Third Reich as a technological, people-friendly paradise enabling Germans to travel the length and breadth of their homeland. The development of the network was extensively covered by newspapers, in newsreels, on radio and on the new medium of television to convey this impression. Very few Germans could afford cars and Hitler's dream of the 'people's car', which became the VW Beetle, was only realised after the end of Nazi rule.

Providing pleasant areas for motorists to stop and rest was part of this overall approach. Hitler is alleged to have influenced the choice of location for what was in effect the world's first motorway service station on the shores of Chiemsee in Bavaria on the Munich to Salzburg route. It was opened on 27 August 1937 with 520 seats, dining space for 350, an outside

British Prime Minister, Neville Chamberlain, and the German Foreign Minister, Joachim von Ribbentrop, visit Rasthaus Chiemsee on the Munich-Salzburg autobahn, September 1938 (Bundesarchiv, unknown)

Buildings of the former Rasthaus Chiemsee which is now a health clinic (Bayerische Landsamt für Denkmalpflege)

terrace able to accommodate over 1,300 people and an outdoor swimming pool; its popularity was so great that closure was forced on several occasions due to overcrowding. The Germans were keen to show it off and the British Prime Minister, Neville Chamberlain, was entertained there in September 1938 during one of his visits to Germany prior to the Munich Agreement. After the war the site was used by the American military as a recreation centre until 2002. The buildings now have monument protection status and, since 2012, one has been used as a health clinic.

Chiemsee itself is no longer a motorway service area but the vast majority of the Reichsautobahn network constructed up to 1941 remains in use. Two years into the war all new motorway construction came to a standstill with resources diverted to the war effort. For most of the war very little private traffic was allowed on the autobahnen which were used for freight traffic – including moving military parts between factories. A few sections were closed as roads and used as military runways and some motorway tunnels became armaments factories (see Chapter Six). Towards the war's end significant damage was done to the motorways both by retreating German forces destroying bridges and intersections attempting to stall the Allied progress, and also by the advancing Allies themselves; many surfaces were found to be inadequate for the weights imposed by convoys of military transport.

The legacy of the Nazis' motorway building programme from 1933 to 1941 is really twofold. Firstly, the Reichsautobahn was the first proper motorway network in the world and many of the technical, aesthetic and other lessons learned in their construction influenced the development of high-speed roads elsewhere. Before and after the war engineers travelled to Germany to see it for themselves.

Among the international visitors was James Drake from Lancashire who was the leading light behind Britain's first section of motorway which was opened near Preston in the 1950s. President Eisenhower is said to have been inspired to start the American interstate highways network as a result of seeing the German autobahnen at the end of the war.

Secondly, post-war Germany was bequeathed the beginnings of a motorway network far more extensive than in any other country, albeit one that was damaged and incomplete in 1945. The motorways built during the Third Reich era constitute about a quarter of the total German motorway network in the twenty-first century.

Of all the structures left by the Nazis, the motorway network is probably the least tainted by association. The motives behind the construction of the Reichsautobahnen were in part political and propagandist; they were part of the same hyperbolic vision for the 'Thousand Year Reich' which created the Prora KdF camp and the Nuremberg Rally Grounds. Significant sections of the motorway network were also constructed using forced labour. These factors, however, were not strong enough counterbalances to the power of pragmatic common sense to make use of this legacy in the rebuilding of Germany after 1945.

The German motorway network has, stage by stage, been expanded and completed. Both governments in a divided Germany resumed motorway building – West Germany more enthusiastically. But the division of the country produced some quirky legacies. Some routes were bisected by the border that divided East and West Germany and other unfinished routes

View of the first motorway service area – Rasthaus Chiemsee from the air, 1937 (Archiv Eckhard Gruber)

Remains of the so-called 'Strecke 46' section of uncompleted motorway near Gmünden am Main – part of an unfinished plan to link Hamburg and Lake Constance (Blueduck4711)

were not completed because the division of the country made them unnecessary.

For example, the so-called Berlinka motorway, originally planned to link Berlin with Königsberg in East Prussia, was split between East Germany, Poland and the Soviet Union. Some segments of the road became virtually 'ghost roads' hardly used by any traffic and were tourist attractions in their own right as examples of Nazi architecture frozen in aspic. Since reunification most of this road, and many other disconnected sections of motorway, have either been upgraded or incorporated into local roads.

This was not inevitable; deep in the woods in the Lower Franconian Forest near Gmünden am Main almost fifty relics remain of a section of motorway started during the Nazi era but never finished. They are bridges, supports and other structures related to *'Strecke 46'* or section forty-six of the planned Hamburg to Lake Constance autobahn. They stretch along a section of over 65km of the originally planned route of the motorway. When the road was completed post-war, as what is now the A7, it was decided to take a different route about 30km further east. Today tourists walk the route of *'Strecke 46'* to see one of the more curious relics of the Third Reich.

HAUS DER KUNST, MUNICH, BAVARIA

It stands on the southern edge of the Englischer Garten, Munich's largest park, and is scheduled to undergo a 60 million Euros redevelopment designed by the British architect David Chipperfield. However, the post-war history of the 'Haus der Kunst' has been marked by controversy about

Haus der Kunst, now a major art gallery of international significance, on the edge of the Englischer Garten in Munich (Andreas von der Au)

whether it should be retained at all given its origins as one of the very first monuments built by the Nazis.

The 'Haus der Deutschen Kunst', 'The House of German Art' as it was originally called, was designed by Paul Ludwig Troost on Hitler's orders and built between 1933 and 1937 on the site of a great glass palace used as an exhibition centre which had been destroyed by fire in 1931. The new building and its purpose were central to Nazi philosophy and propaganda and it played a key role in the Third Reich's attempts to define and control cultural taste across Germany. It was opened on 18 July 1937 to show off what the Nazis regarded as Germany's greatest art with its first exhibition entitled the 'Great German Art Exhibition'.

This exhibition contained traditional landscapes and classical art featuring the human form and other works of art conforming to the Aryan ideals of the Nazi regime. It was repeated each year throughout the remainder of the Third Reich and its opening in the main hall of the 'Haus der Deutschen Kunst' was a major propaganda occasion for the Nazi leadership.

This opening exhibition was designed to be in marked contrast to an exhibition of so-called 'Degenerate Art' staged by the Nazis not far away in Munich at the Institute of Archaeology featuring the work of many artists, some of them Jewish, viewed by the regime as 'degenerate'. These included many artists now regarded as some of the greatest of the twentieth century including Marc Chagall, Paul Klee and Wassily Kandinsky. More than a million people visited this exhibition – three times the numbers who visited the 'Great German Art Exhibition'. Visitors appear to have been not only Nazi supporters and others who agreed with the official view of modern art as degenerate, but also people who had realised that this might be the last time to see modern art of this kind in Germany. The exhibition toured across Germany and was seen by a further million people.

When the Americans marched into Munich at the end of April 1945 much of the city lay in ruins but the Haus der Deutschen Kunst was largely intact. The last 'Great German Art Exhibition' had been held there the previous year and, as late as February 1945, Hitler was apparently ordering preparations for the next such exhibition later that year.

In another example of the pragmatism of utilizing Nazi buildings the Americans immediately converted it into a club for service personnel to include cooking facilities, a restaurant, a dance hall and several shops. Basketball courts were laid out on what had been the exhibition floors and jazz bands performed in the hall where the Nazis had once condemned modern culture.

In 1946 the building was renamed 'Haus der Kunst', and parts of it began to be used again for temporary art exhibitions including the display of Munich's own art collection. Many of the exhibitions staged there in the early post-war years deliberately featured modern art which was seen as a form of denazification of the building. A Picasso retrospective in 1955 featuring his painting 'Guernica', a symbol of antifascism in art, was shown in Germany for the first time. Throughout the next thirty years the 'Haus der Kunst' became a major venue for international art exhibitions including many of the works of artists labelled 'degenerate' during the Third Reich. A series of structural changes, meanwhile, took place in the building which

Haus der Deutschen Kunst in Munich – one of the first monumental buildings constructed by the Nazis and opened in July 1937 (Bundesarchiv, unknown)

had the effect of further denazifying it. This approach was seen by many as a form of atonement for the origins of the gallery.

It was only in the late 1980s, partly because the building was by then in need of serious renovation, that a debate started about its future. This coincided with more open consideration about the fate of Nazi architecture. Many people wanted to see the Nazi structure demolished but eventually the Bavarian Government decided on a partial renovation which was completed in 1993. In 1996, for the first time, there was a small exhibition in the 'Haus der Kunst' detailing its own history. More recently, since the start of a programme of so-called 'Critical Reconstruction' some of the physical changes have been reversed and the original features of the building have once again been exposed. This has been part of a process of coming to terms with the origins of the building as well as its necessary development as an international exhibition space – a process set to continue with the Chipperfield-led renovation expected to start by 2016.

As a footnote, the Americans may have moved out in 1956 but there is now an upmarket nightclub called P1 occupying part of the building. The name derives from its original American users – an abbreviation of the address of 1 Prinzregentenstrasse.

THINGSTÄTTEN

The Nazis perpetuated the idea of the 'Volk' community – the idea that all Germans, irrespective of their social status or their regional loyalties, were part of a common culture underpinned by quasi-spiritual roots deep in German history. Joseph Goebbels was also an exponent of the so-called 'Blut und Boden' (Blood and Soil) philosophy which emphasised the connections between the German people and their land.

One product of these rather vaguely defined ideas were the theatrical performances 'Thingspiele' staged in amphitheatres (Thingstätten) harking back to the old Germanic and Nordic concept of the 'Thing' – outdoor gatherings of people to celebrate their common heritage. Specially written productions were to be put on at a network of Thingstätten across the Reich to provide officially sanctioned entertainment for the masses.

The first of these amphitheatres opened in Brandberge in Halle in 1934 in what was supposed to be the beginning of a network of over 400 across Germany. In fact only around forty were ever built. The Nazi leadership appears to have rather lost interest in the idea. Insufficient productions were written and, above all, the idea of sitting outside in the often chilly German weather watching dramas of dubious interest was unsurprisingly not that popular. After a few years, the amphitheatres were designated as more general open air theatres putting on conventional dramas or were used to celebrate events like the summer solstice.

The Berlin Waldbühne was originally built as the Dietrich-Eckart-Bühne for the 1936 Olympic Games and is still in use as an outdoor arena (Gryffindor)

Ruins of Brandberge Thingstätte – the first open air arena built under the Third Reich and originally intended to be part of a network of 200 across Germany (Milena Waleska)

The Dietrich-Eckart-Bühne on the Berlin Olympic site just before the outbreak of war in 1939 (Bundesarchiv, A.Frankl)

Heiligenberg Thingstätte, Heidelberg remains like many Thingstätten across Germany and is now part of a public park (Bishkekrocks)

Nevertheless, one of the venues did play a central role in the 1936 Berlin Olympics (see Chapter Four). The Dietrich-Eckart-Bühne, designed by Werner March, was built on the Olympic site in Berlin. A production of a specially commissioned drama, Eberhard Wolfgang Möller's Frankenburger Würfelspiel, was premiered on 2 August, the day after the opening of the Games. The amphitheatre was used for a number of Olympic events including boxing. Afterwards, like other Thingstätten, it was used more widely for choral and opera performances and played a role in the 1937 celebration of the 700th anniversary of the founding of Berlin.

Despite their origins as arenas of Nazi 'worship', a significant number of Thingstätten remain. The Dietrich-Eckart-Bühne in Berlin, now known as the Waldbühne, holds 22,000 people, has become a key venue for concerts and has hosted many of the most famous names of rock music since 1945. These include Jimi Hendrix, Eric Clapton, Barbra Streisand and, perhaps most notoriously, the Rolling Stones whose concert there in September 1965 ended in a riot with major damage to the arena.

The ruins of the first Thingstätte at Brandberge are designated a historical monument but many others, including the largely intact arena in Heidelberg, are still complete and used as public parks.

CARINHALL, SCHORFHEIDE FOREST, BRANDENBURG

In the middle of the Schorfheide Forest, close to the town of Eberswalde about fifty miles from Berlin, two entrance gates stand by the roadside. It is easy to miss them and nothing indicates their origins or significance. They are, however, virtually all that remains of an important Third Reich relic – the home of one of the most influential members of the Nazi elite.

Carinhall was built in stages from 1933 and designed by Werner March, architect of much of the Berlin Olympic site, as a grand hunting lodge for Hermann Göring who had purchased the land for his country retreat. The house was later dedicated as an official residence and its considerable upkeep costs paid by the state. After several enlargements it contained a bowling alley, a cinema, a swimming pool, and his vast model train set.

It was named after Göring's first wife, Carin Fock, a Swedish divorcee whom he had married in 1923 but who died after a heart attack in 1931 at the age of forty-three in her native Stockholm. Göring was devastated by her death, named his country retreat after her and filled the house with pictures and mementoes of her. In 1934 her remains were brought to Germany and reinterred in a specially built mausoleum in the grounds of Carinhall. Hitler was among the leading Nazis who attended the ceremony.

Göring remarried and his second wife Emmy and their daughter, Edda, who was born in 1938, lived there for much of the war. Carinhall became the destination of much looted art treasure.

Today Carinhall does not exist. As the Russians advanced towards Berlin in early 1945 Göring ordered its destruction to prevent it falling into Soviet

The surviving gates of Carinhall in the Schorfheide Forest – the country retreat of Reichsmarshall Hermann Göring (Brandenburg Landamt)

Hermann Göring welcoming guests in 1942 to Carinhall which was named after his first wife, Carin Fock (Bundesarchiv, unknown)

hands and it was dynamited by the Luftwaffe in late April. Göring, his wife and daughter, had already retreated to Berchtesgaden with the looted art. He committed suicide in October 1946 on the eve of his planned execution after being found guilty of war crimes at the Nuremberg Trials.

After the war the East German army blew up what remained of the buildings at Carinhall. Some of the remains of Göring's first wife, Carin, were discovered in 1951 in the grounds and were returned to Sweden where they were reburied. In 1991 treasure hunters found more remains which were also sent to Sweden where they were DNA tested and confirmed as hers. The Brandenburg *Land* Government, worried about the site becoming a Neo-Nazi shrine, ordered the destruction of the remains of her tomb in 1999.

BERCHTESGADEN AND THE OBERSALZBERG, BAVARIA

Many homes of the most important Nazi leaders were on the Obersalzberg Mountain near Berchtesgaden in the most southerly corner of Germany in the Bavarian Mountains. Like Carinhall nearly all of these, which made up the mountain retreats and southern command headquarters of the Third Reich leadership on the Obersalzberg, have disappeared. Most were bombed at the very end of the Second World War or later destroyed by the occupying Americans or by the German authorities. Berchtesgaden and the Obersalzberg, nevertheless, remain inextricably linked to the Nazi era – an

Hitler with Hermann Göring, Martin Bormann and Baldur von Shirach at the Berghof, Obersalzberg, 1936 (Bundesarchiv, unknown)

Haus Wachenfeld, later to be renamed the Berghof, with Nazi flag 1934 (Erich Wilhelm Krüger)

association which is now acknowledged by a Documentation Centre which draws hundreds of thousands of visitors to the area each year.

The Nazis' love affair with the Obersalzberg began in the 1920s. Hitler is thought to have first visited the area after his release from prison after serving his sentence for his part in the failed Munich Beer Hall Putsch. He first rented a house there and, later in 1933 when he became Chancellor, bought what later became the Berghof. Existing property owners were forced to sell as the Nazi leadership bought or built houses there to be close to the Führer and the seat of power. The area became more than just a collection of homes and was in effect the southern seat of government and then of wartime command. It fitted well with Nazi ideals as it was rural, in Bavaria, and the birthplace and spiritual home of the movement.

In fact many Nazi relics do remain. The most conspicuous of these could, possibly, be visited without realising its origins. During the summer months there is an almost constant stream of coaches and buses taking people up the winding road to the carpark of the Eagle's Nest tearoom. From the carpark at the top of this road, visitors walk along a 100m tunnel carved out inside the mountain and then take a lift inside the mountain to reach the tearoom perched on top of the hillside. This, however, is no ordinary lift as it must be one of the best appointed in the world with brass plated sides, leather interior and elaborate fittings. On leaving the lift a visitor could be forgiven for thinking this is just another panoramic view across the mountains of southern Bavaria and Austria.

The Eagle's Nest on the Obersalzberg – a fiftieth birthday present for Adolf Hitler and now an Alpine tearoom (Colin Philpott)

*The well-appointed lift leading to the Eagle's Nest, one of the few Nazi buildings
untouched by Allied bombing on the Obersalzberg in April 1945 (Colin Philpott)*

There is little or nothing to suggest that the Eagle's Nest was in fact built as a fiftieth birthday present for Hitler from the Nazi party in a project masterminded by Martin Bormann. The Kehlsteinhaus, its German name taken from the name of the hill where it is perched, was completed in the summer of 1938 and formally presented to the Führer on his birthday on 20 April 1939. The whole project, particularly the access road which covered 6km involved five tunnels and climbed 800m, was a great engineering feat.

Apparently, however, Hitler was a rather ungrateful recipient of such a grand birthday present. He is thought only to have visited it ten times and never stayed long. Despite its prominence, the Eagle's Nest survived Allied bombing and was also spared the planned demolition of other structures on the Obersalzberg in the 1950s – probably because its tourist potential was realised. It is now run by a trust and its profits are used for charitable purposes.

Other remaining relics from the Third Reich on the Obersalzberg include the Hotel zum Türken. Prior to the Nazis' arrival on the mountain it was a successful hotel but the owner was forced to sell. The building became used as a headquarters for the security service which guarded the Führer and was severely damaged by Allied bombing at the end of the war. The family of the original pre-Nazi owners, however, fought a long battle after the war and eventually repurchased and rebuilt the hotel which remains in operation today. Like almost all the buildings on the mountain it was connected to the others by a network of underground tunnels which can still be visited by hotel guests.

The house containing Albert Speer's architectural studio also remains and is now a private residence. In Berchtesgaden itself there are three notable remains from the Nazi era. The railway station was rebuilt during the Third Reich because it was the frequent arrival point for Nazi leaders and for visiting dignitaries. It was damaged in the war but rebuilt again in the 1950s maintaining the 1930s style. The Nazi-era Post Office also survives and a disused railway tunnel, not far from the station, can still be seen; a train containing part of Göring's looted art collection was stored there towards the end of the war.

Many of the most iconic Nazi-era buildings on the Obersalzberg have gone. Perhaps the most famous was Hitler's house, the Berghof. Originally Haus Wachenfeld, Hitler rented it during a stay in the 1920s but bought it in 1933 and enlarged it. With its panoramic windows affording sweeping views of the mountains and its balcony, it was the place immortalised in many photographs and film images – Hitler with Eva Braun, Hitler with his dog, and Hitler with a range of famous guests. These included the Italian leader, Benito Mussolini, the Duke of Windsor who had abdicated as King of England and, perhaps most famously, the British Prime Minister Neville Chamberlain who was entertained there by Hitler during discussions prior to the Munich Agreement.

One of the few surviving remains of more than fifty Nazi-era buildings on the Obersalzberg (Colin Philpott)

Berchtesgaden Station rebuilt in the 1950s in 1930s National Socialist style (unknown)

Hitler greets British Prime Minister, Neville Chamberlain at the Berghof, September 1938 during discussions which led to the Munich Agreement (Bundesarchiv, unknown)

The Platterhof was a hostel for the many visitors who flocked to the Obersalzberg during the Nazi era to catch a glimpse of the Führer. After the war it became a hotel for American servicemen, the General Walker Hotel, but after the final American withdrawal from Germany it was demolished in 2001. Gone also are the various houses of other Nazi leaders including those of Göring and Bormann. More than fifty Nazi buildings had been located on the Obersalzberg including guesthouses, a theatre and SS barracks.

The events of one day, Wednesday 25 April 1945, explain why all but half a dozen of these are no longer standing. More than 300 British Lancaster bombers, supported by over 200 US planes and others from Canada and Australia pounded the Obersalzberg for over an hour. Only six people died in the raid but the damage to property was immense. Hitler's Berghof, the SS barracks, the Hotel zum Türken, the Platterhof and Bormann and Göring's houses were all either destroyed or badly damaged. Astonishingly, the Eagle's Nest on top of the Kehlstein survived.

Earlier in the war Berchtesgaden had not been a bombing target; it was of little strategic importance and was beyond the reach of most Allied bombers until later. The raid on 25 April is thought to have been mainly

Extensive damage to the Berghof after Allied raids on the Obersalzberg on 25 April 1945 (unknown)

The Nazi Documentation Centre on the Obersalzberg built to explain the role of the area in the Third Reich story and opened in 1999 (Colin Philpott)

motivated not by a desire to strike a symbolic target but because there was a belief among the Allied command that the Germans might make a last ditch stand there.

Decisions about the future of the Nazi sites on the Obersalzberg after the war were first made by the occupying Americans and, later, the Bavarian authorities. The ruins of Hitler's Berghof were reputed to have been left untouched until the early 1950s as a warning of the dangers of Nazism. They were, however, demolished later and today only one side wall remains. As the property of leading Nazis and of the Nazi party was transferred to the *Land* Governments it ultimately fell to the Bavarian Government to decide what to do with much of the area.

In 1999, on the site of one of the former Nazi guesthouses, a Documentation Centre was opened which, like those at Nuremberg and elsewhere, tells the story of Nazi Germany and the particular part played by the Obersalzberg. The Bavarian *Land* Government has recently approved plans to extend the centre by adding a new building and developing a seminar centre. Of around 170,000 annual visitors to the centre about a quarter come from outside Germany.

SUMMARY

Many of the buildings and sites discussed in this chapter not only survived the collapse of Nazism but were actively maintained and developed in the post-war years. This is perhaps not surprising because most were rather useful. The motivation for building them had been part of Nazi ideology but these were not buildings or places associated with their terror. On the contrary many were specifically designed by the Nazis to be part of everyday life for German people. A motorway network, a grand art gallery in Munich and a large hotel in the Bavarian hills were legacies that post-war Germany could utilise. Forty or so amphitheatres around the country were maybe less useful but they could in many cases blend back into the natural surroundings from which they had been created.

The private houses of the Nazi leadership were perhaps never going to survive the end of the war; although those on the Obersalzberg may have been bombed by the Allies for mainly military purposes they would probably have been demolished anyway for symbolic reasons. Indeed, the ruins that remained of those not obliterated by bombing were eventually torn down.

The Prora-Rügen holiday complex on the Baltic Coast remains the most intriguing of these sites. It represents the ultimate triumph of pragmatism over symbolism with the current renovation of the holiday blocks that straddle almost 5km of coastline. This is returning them to their originally intended use as places to take a holiday, albeit one stripped of its Nazi ideology.

Chapter Three

Enforcement
(Durchsetzung)

Dachau Memorial – Dachau had opened in March 1933 as the first permanent concentration camp established during the Third Reich (Colin Philpott)

PREAMBLE

The litany of concentration camp names which resonates down the years can almost anaesthetise us to the magnitude of the crimes committed at these places. The names are now so familiar that they trip off the tongue almost too easily. Auschwitz, Bergen-Belsen, Treblinka, Sachsenhausen, Dachau and many, many more – in fact an estimated 15,000 camps of one sort or another were built in Nazi occupied Europe.

Terror, intimidation, extra-judicial murder and later industrial-scale genocide, underpinned by a virulently racist ideology, were key characteristics of Nazi Germany. The places where these horrors took place have become the focus of much of the public remembrance of the evils of the Nazis in general and of the Holocaust in particular.

At this stage, during the peacetime Nazi years, our focus is on the places associated with enforcing control within the Reich. Embedding National Socialism in the German psyche through propaganda and material benefits was important but so was fear and terror and, in this chapter, we examine some of the places that played a key role in this.

Within weeks of taking power early in 1933, the very first permanent concentration camp was opened at Dachau near Munich to deal with political opponents. Much of the internal terror which became a hallmark of Nazi Germany was masterminded from behind the grim façade of the Gestapo Headquarters in Berlin. The Nazi war machine was planned from the new Air Ministry building in Berlin. Three military academies, or Ordensburgen, were set up around the Reich to train the Nazi elite. Finally the virtual destruction of the Reichstag (the German Parliament) by fire was a pivotal event in securing the Nazi hold on power.

DACHAU CONCENTRATION CAMP, DACHAU, BAVARIA

Its surroundings and ambience are highly relevant to a visitor to Dachau. The town of Dachau, about 20km north-west of Munich, is now part of what the Germans call the 'Speckgürtel', the 'bacon-belt' – in other words the affluent suburbs of the Bavarian capital. It feels very genteel and suggests twenty-first century German prosperity. Yet, amidst this quiet town, lie the remains of the place where, in many ways, the Nazi reign of terror across Germany, and much of Europe, began.

Dachau was probably chosen as the site for the first permanent Nazi concentration camp because of its proximity to the spiritual home of the movement, Munich. It was opened by Heinrich Himmler on 22 March 1933 on the site of a disused munitions factory within two months of Hitler coming to power. Its first prisoners were around 200 political opponents of the regime taken into 'protective custody' to 'restore order'. The scope of its activities and the range of its prisoners gradually expanded. Homosexuals, Jehovah's Witnesses, clergy, writers and other intellectuals, Sinti, Roma and, of course, both German and Austrian Jews were sent there as were prisoners of war. Dachau was run by the SS and became a model for subsequent concentration camps.

The Dachau concentration camp site first established as a memorial as a result of pressure from survivors and the families of those who died there (Colin Philpott)

Barracks at Dachau Concentration Camp shortly after its liberation in April 1945 (Sidney Blau, US Army)

Dachau was never an extermination camp in the way that Auschwitz and many others were but it was a place of torture, forced labour (mainly in armaments factories), medical experimentation and much more besides. It is estimated that over 200,000 people from thirty-four different nations were sent to Dachau and its 100 or so nearby subsidiary camps during its twelve-year history and that as many as 40,000 were killed or died during their captivity there. The overall treatment of US and British prisoners of war by Germany was generally in accordance with the Geneva Convention but Soviet prisoners of war were not afforded the same treatment and many ended up in concentration camps including Dachau. An estimated 5,000 Soviet prisoners of war held there were shot.

Even as late as March 1945, with the war lost, new prisoners were being sent to Dachau as the Germans moved inmates from camps near the front line to those further away. An estimated 10,000 of Dachau's 30,000 inmates died between the autumn of 1944 and the end of the war in May 1945. Many were victims of malnutrition or one of the many typhoid outbreaks that occurred. Well into April 1945 Heinrich Himmler turned down a suggestion by the commandant of Dachau that the camp should be surrendered to the advancing Allies. Instead Himmler ordered that the remaining inmates either be marched to the Alps or murdered at Dachau if they were unable to travel. Thousands died in the last weeks before Dachau was liberated by American troops on 29 April 1945.

The discoveries by Allied troops as they reached Dachau are well documented but the appalling conditions had left many of the inmates at

Bodies discovered at Dachau, April 1945 – an estimated 40,000 people died at Dachau either executed or through malnutrition, disease or as a result of medical experiments (US National Archives, unknown)

the point of death and many died in the weeks after liberation. Some prisoners turned on their guards and killed them and a military investigation found that American soldiers had summarily shot some of Dachau's SS guards during the liberation after they had surrendered.

After its liberation Dachau continued as a detention centre – now with Germans being held on suspicion of war crimes. SS guards and Nazi officials were imprisoned there awaiting trial and it was only three years later that the site was handed over to the Bavarian authorities. A housing development was subsequently built to house refugees and homeless people.

Through the 1950s and into the 1960s pressure grew from survivors and families of those who had died in Dachau to establish a memorial there. In 1960 a chapel was dedicated on the site and in 1962 the Bavarian

Pile of prisoners' clothes at the time of the liberation of Dachau in April, 1945 – many more prisoners died after the liberation through disease (US National Archives, unknown)

Government and the committee representing survivors, the *Comite International de Dachau,* agreed to establish a proper memorial on the site. In 1965 a new Documentation Centre was opened and the former camp was formally established as a memorial site.

The establishment of a memorial at Dachau was mirrored by similar developments at other concentration camp sites across Germany and beyond. The twenty years taken was a reflection of two things.

Many camps were destroyed by the Allies or by the retreating Germans themselves. Many former concentration camps were, however, pressed into service as camps by the Allies either to hold suspected war criminals or, later, German refugees expelled from Eastern Europe. Only after those uses had expired did thinking start about the fate of these emotionally-charged places.

Furthermore the Allied occupation powers and, later, the post-war German authorities were not initially particularly interested in tackling the issue which was only pursued as a result of survivor pressure. For the

Americans and the British the priorities were dealing with the Cold War threat from the former ally, the Soviet Union, and building up the West German economy. For the Germans, as they regained the levers of power in the 1950s, confronting the Nazi past was too difficult – particularly in conservative Bavaria. But for the concerted and long-running pressure from survivors of Dachau and the families of those who had died there the site would almost certainly not have been established as a memorial in the 1960s.

Since then, the Dachau site has been changed a number of times. In addition to a central memorial where the main roll-call area once stood there are now two reconstructed barracks and recreated foundations to mark the location of thirty other barracks buildings. The original barracks were demolished but not until the 1960s once they had served their usefulness in housing refugees. Also visible are the gatehouse, the watch towers and the crematorium; the maintenance building where the main Documentation Centre is housed and four religious chapels are also on the site. In November 2014 the iconic 'Arbeit macht frei' (Work sets you free) sign on the camp gates at Dachau was stolen.

Polish prisoners toasting liberation from Dachau by US forces on 29 April 1945 (Arland Mausser, US National Archives and Records Administration)

The preserved crematorium building at Dachau – part of the memorial established on the former concentration camp site (Colin Philpott)

Plans for the future development include bringing the herb garden, where prisoners were used as forced labour, into the memorial site as currently this is outside the area permitted to visitors. There are also plans for new exhibitions in one of the reconstituted barracks.

Dachau is not alone. Elsewhere in Germany, many of the main concentration camp sites are commemorated in some way either through a documentation centre or a simpler memorial. In most cases these memorials were established in the 1960s – usually through pressure from survivors. Now the costs of most of these so-called 'victim sites' are supported by the Federal as well as by *Land* governments.

I have visited Dachau twice and the simplicity of the memorial site is very moving. However chilling the recital of terror in the Documentation Centre, the scale of events at Dachau is best conveyed by walking around the bare but extensive grounds and seeing the reconstruction marking where thirty barracks once stood.

Visiting Dachau is also disturbing as an act of what has become known as 'dark tourism' – the visiting of places where bad things happened. One of the occasions I visited was during the summer of 2006 when the football World Cup was taking place in Germany. People in the football shirts of many nationalities were including Dachau on their tourist trail whilst in the country to watch the World Cup. On another occasion my visit coincided with a very large group of loud and disruptive students who did not seem to see the need to respect the place. It appeared to be just another stop on their journey.

Dachau provokes feelings that are both uncomfortable and reverential. The discomfort arises from questioning the motive for undertaking the visit. It is also a place of genuine remembrance. Professor John Lennon, with his colleague Professor Malcolm Foley, coined the phrase 'dark tourism' in the 1990s and he has visited and studied many similar sites across the world. He accepts that places like Dachau have become 'commodified' and are now part of tourist itineraries. He maintains, however, that this has merit in that some visitors at least will engage more deeply with such sites and the history they represent. He also believes that, for some, visiting a place like Dachau may offer their only learning experience about this element of a darker past.

The attitude of the people of Dachau, however, towards the camp and the memorial site is perhaps even more interesting than that of touring visitors. The general view is that for years local people ignored it. It was clearly a very uncomfortable part of their history and often portrayed as being someone else's history. Dachau managed to convince itself that it was a victim of the Nazis – the town had not asked to have the camp there. In the 1930s, however, Dachau was a relatively poor town and many local people derived economic benefit from the camp which, of course, adds to the discomfort now felt; even changing the town's name has been discussed.

Recently a much more open debate about the camp and the memorial has taken place with most local people now accepting it as part of their

'Never Again' Memorial – centrepiece of the Dachau memorial site (Colin Philpott)

history. On her 2014 visit there the German Chancellor, Angela Merkel criticized her fellow countrymen for having turned a blind eye, and indeed acquiesced, to Dachau and to Nazi terror more generally – something which would have been inconceivable from a German leader twenty years previously.

GÖRING'S AIR MINISTRY, BERLIN

Detlev-Rohwedder-Haus, in the centre of Berlin – the home of the German Federal Finance Ministry (Hans Oberlack)

This is now Detlev-Rohwedder-Haus, an imposing structure along the Wilhelmstrasse in the heart of Berlin, housing the German Federal Finance Ministry. At first glance it is just another administrative building in the German capital but, like many state buildings erected in Germany in the 1930s, its interesting history is at the heart of four different systems of government across almost eighty years.

The building was constructed between early 1935 and the summer of 1936 to house the newly created Reich Air Ministry. Headed by Hermann Göring this new government department was set up by the Nazis in recognition of the growing military importance of air power. Military aviation had previously been supervised by a department of the army. This changed with the creation of the Reichsluftfahrtministerium and marked the beginning of the creation of the Luftwaffe which was to play such a significant role in the German war effort.

The headquarters of this new body were in the imposing classical style favoured by the Nazis. The architect was Ernst Sagebiel who also designed Tempelhof Airport (see Chapter Four). The building contained nearly 3,000 rooms over seven storeys, with a total floor area of more than 100,000 square metres. 4,000 people worked there and the frontage stretched for over 250m with its end wall adorned by a huge swastika and eagle.

It was within these walls that Hermann Göring masterminded the creation of the *Luftwaffe* as German rearmament gathered pace in the second half of the 1930s. After the outbreak of the war in 1939 the demands on the Ministry increased and, by all accounts, Göring's control of it was haphazard. Control of aviation manufacture was later given to Albert Speer and production improved but too late to change the course of the conflict.

The building itself, though, survived the intense bombing of Berlin with only relatively minor damage and, despite its leading role in the Nazi war machine, it was immediately pressed into service by the Soviet occupation forces into whose zone it fell. The building was repaired, the Nazi insignia removed and it became the headquarters of the German Economic Commission, effectively the leading organisation in the Soviet zone, providing a new life for a grand building and its second use. In 1949 the creation of East Germany as the German Democratic Republic was marked in a ceremony inside the building; this took place in the room which had been the original Third Reich Ehrensaal or Honour Hall but which had had been converted into the Festsaal.

For the next forty years, the building was at the heart of the East German government machine and renamed the Haus der Ministerien housing various departments – its third use. Having served as an important location for the one dictatorship it then served another. Perhaps that caused the building to become the main focus of the uprising against the East German state in 1953 – one which was ruthlessly suppressed.

Reichsluftfahrtministerium or Göring's Air Ministry, 1938 established as the Nazis recognised the importance of building up their military power in the air (Bundesarchiv, unknown)

After German reunification in 1990, having served two dictatorships and an occupier, it became a key location for a democratic regime. It housed the body that privatised the former state enterprises of the GDR and was renamed Detlev-Rohwedder-Haus in 1992 in honour of the chairman of that organisation who had been murdered by the German terrorist group, the Red Army Faction. Today the building houses the German Finance Ministry which moved there from Bonn after reunification.

The Air Ministry building is another example of a Nazi-era building which, for largely pragmatic reasons, has been preserved and put to new uses since 1945 and which has lost much of its Nazi taint. In 1945 Berlin well-designed buildings suitable for use by government agencies were in short supply so its survival is perhaps unsurprising.

ORDENSBURG VOGELSANG, SCHLEIDEN, NORTH-RHINE WESTPHALIA
ORDENSBURG SONTHOFEN, ALLGAU, BAVARIA
ORDENSBURG KRÖSSINSEE, POMERANIA, POLAND

Like the Air Ministry in Berlin three imposing structures which housed the military academies established by the Nazis to train the young elite of the Third Reich have all survived the intervening eighty years. This endurance, like Göring's Berlin Luftwaffe Headquarters, is the result of pure pragmatism.

In 1933 Hitler announced that he wanted a network of centres established to train the Third Reich's military elite of the future. Recruits had to be between twenty-five and thirty years old, confirmed Nazis, and

The imposing structure of NS-Ordensburg Vogelsang still dominates the skyline near Schleiden in North-Rhine Westphalia (VoWo)

Hitler at NS-Ordensburg Vogelsang in North-Rhine Westphalia – one of three elite academies established by the Nazis (Bundesarchiv, unknown)

of pure Aryan stock. Four centres were planned with each specialising in a different area of education. They were known as NS-Ordensburgen and recruits were to spend a year at each. The regime was hard and included mornings of study, afternoons of sport, physical education and military training, and more lessons in the evenings.

Three of the centres, Vogelsang, Sonthofen and Krössinsee, were built and operated as intended. The fourth, Marienburg at Malbork Castle in what is now Poland, was a pre-existing building which was used for rallies and events but never operated in the same way as the other three.

Ordensburg Vogelsang in North-Rhine Westphalia specialised in teaching the Nazi ideas on race. It was planned on a vast scale although some plans went unrealised as a result of the outbreak of war. The centre included a community house, dormitories, extensive sports facilities and a Thingplatz auditorium but a planned Haus des Wissens, or library, was only partially completed. The complex operated from 1936 but, after the war started, it was handed over to the army and used as barracks.

After the war many surviving buildings were repaired and the area was used as a military training area by the West German Bundeswehr until 2006. The buildings can now be visited by tourists and they form part of the Eifel National Park. NS-Ordensburg Vogelsang is one of the largest surviving Nazi architectural relics anywhere.

Recruits marching in 1937 at NS-Ordensburg Vogelsang, which specialised in teaching Nazi ideas on race (Bundesarchiv, unknown)

Model of NS-Ordensburg Sonthofen which specialised in military training, administration and diplomacy (Bundesarchiv, unknown)

NS-Ordensburg Krössinsee in Pomerania is now in Poland and is still in use today by the Polish Army (Bundesarchiv, unknown)

NS-Ordensburg Sonthofen was built in 1934 in the Oberallgäu region of the Bavarian Alps and it specialised in military training, administration and diplomacy. After the war it was used first by French troops, then by the US Army and from 1956 by the Bundeswehr. It remains a military facility although on a smaller scale and is preserved as a historic site.

The third such centre was NS-Ordensburg Krössinsee near the city of Falkenburg, now Zlocieniec in Pomerania in Poland. Opened in 1936, it specialised in the development of character. Today it is used as a military facility by the Polish Army.

The historical significance of these sites is recognised in all three cases, particularly in the two sites still in Germany which visitors can access. As with many other Nazi buildings, their survival is again an example of pragmatism. These were useful, largely undamaged by war and were needed post-1945. Their original purpose was to indoctrinate the Nazi leaders of the future and, within their walls, a generation of young Germans was taught some of the most heinous Nazi ideas. They were not, however, sites associated with terror or genocide and consequently easier to assimilate into post-war life.

GESTAPO HEADQUARTERS, BERLIN

The post-war fate of the NS-Ordensburgen complexes is in marked contrast to the buildings that once stood on what was then Prinz-Albrecht-Strasse in the centre of Berlin. If there is one place that can be said to be the very nerve centre of Nazi terror and repression this was it. Number 8, Prinz-Albrecht-Strasse can rightly be described as one of the most notorious addresses in history.

The building had originally been the School of Applied Arts but in 1933 it was acquired and turned into the headquarters of both the Gestapo and the SS and, later, the Reich Security Service which brought together the various agencies of repression which existed in the Third Reich. Gestapo was the short name for the 'Geheime Staatspolizei', the secret police, which, under the leadership of Heinrich Himmler, became the main agency of terror in Nazi Germany and later in Nazi-occupied territories. The SS, or Schutzstaffel literally 'protection squad', grew from a small paramilitary unit originally used to protect Hitler and other Nazi leaders before they came to power. It was to become a major military and terror organisation of more than a million people and was responsible for the majority of Nazi war crimes.

Headquarters of the Gestapo, Prinz-Albrecht-Strasse, Berlin, 1933 – the Nazi terror machine was masterminded here (Bundesarchiv, unknown)

'Topography of Terror' Documentation Centre, Berlin built on the site of the former Gestapo Headquarters (Topography of Terror Centre)

The Prinz-Albrecht-Strasse building was both an administrative headquarters and an interrogation centre. In cellars beneath the building, the Gestapo employed a range of interrogation methods on German citizens suspected of opposition to the regime. Many Gestapo victims resulted from denunciations by fellow citizens and it is said that passers-by on the street could regularly hear screams coming from the cells.

The building was extensively damaged by Allied bombing and the ruins of this most notorious of Nazi structures were later demolished. The street constituted the boundary between the American and Soviet occupation zones of Berlin and the site of the Gestapo Headquarters was right alongside the Berlin Wall which was built by the East Germans to divide Berlin in 1961.

Today, however, a shiny new building stands where the Gestapo building once stood and the street, now fully reopened and renamed Niederkirchnerstrasse, is, incidentally, very close to one of very few remaining sections of the Berlin Wall. The 'Topography of Terror' Documentation Centre tells of the role of the Gestapo, the SS and the other agencies of Nazi terror. The centre was opened in 2010 but the first public acknowledgement of the history of the site had taken place almost a quarter of a century earlier before German reunification. East and West Berliners had collaborated to create a temporary exhibition on the excavated site of the former Gestapo cells – an outdoor display protected by a canopy to document events on the site.

A foundation was established, post reunification, to care for the site; work started on building a permanent exhibition but was delayed by

Walking route at the 'Topography of Terror' which includes views of the basement where torture took place during the Third Reich era (Topography of Terror Centre)

financial problems and ongoing debates about how the site should be commemorated. One dispute concerned the fate of the basement cells where torture had taken place. Some argued that they should not be excavated but others disagreed. Some amateur archaeologists, meanwhile, even started digging to uncover these particularly chilling places of terror.

The Centre is now supported by both the Federal and Berlin governments. It contains exhibitions detailing the story of Nazi terror and also a fifteen 'station' tour of the site detailing specific remains of the building, including the basement cells, and their significance. There is a strong emphasis on the victims and on the stories of specific sufferers.

Visiting the 'Topography of Terror' represented for me one of the most powerful experiences at any Nazi site in Germany. The Germans refer to 'perpetrator sites' and 'victim sites' yet this is both. It details the horror of torture, of terror, and of the bureaucratic, institutionalised nature of the Third Reich terror machine. It provides a focus on the thinking of those who planned and executed that machine while treating the victims as more than nameless statistics. They are brought to life as real people and the geography is important. Not only is this the actual site from which these crimes were planned, and where so many were committed, but it is the very heart of the German capital. Here is a country detailing an episode of its own moral degradation just a stone's throw from its seat of government and cheek by jowl with its new prosperity; the visitor is left both shocked and heartened.

REICHSTAG BUILDING AND KROLL OPERA HOUSE, BERLIN

This story is mostly about buildings and public spaces that the Nazis created or buildings and locations they appropriated or acquired. A discussion of the legacy of the architecture of the Third Reich would, however, be incomplete without reference to buildings they tore down or deliberately destroyed.

The wanton devastation of 'Kristallnacht' – 9 and 10 November 1938 – when over 1,000 synagogues were destroyed and more than 7,000 Jewish businesses were attacked probably constitutes the single most shocking act of state-sponsored destruction of the property of its own citizens in modern history. Attacks on Jews and their buildings were, of course, not confined to that night and were part of a theme of destruction undertaken by the Nazis against people and objects they considered 'un-German' – including the notorious burning of books and destruction of works of art.

The single most iconic building in Germany to be all but destroyed during the Nazi era was the very heart and symbol of German government and its fragile democracy – the Reichstag.

The seat of Germany's fragile democracy during the Weimar Republic – the Reichstag in 1932 (Bundesarchiv, unknown)

The Reichstag well alight on the evening of 27 February 1933 – the Nazis used the fire as a pretext for violent anti-Communist persecution (US National Archives and Records Administration, unknown)

On the night of 27 February 1933, less than a month after Adolf Hitler had been appointed Chancellor, fire broke out in the Reichstag building. When fire crews arrived the building was well alight and, once it was under control, the damage was found to be extensive. Marinus van der Lubbe, a young Dutch communist, was arrested at the site. He and four other leading Communists subsequently went on trial charged with arson and with attempting to overthrow the government. The four were acquitted but van der Lubbe was found guilty and guillotined in January 1934.

Van der Lubbe claimed that he started the fire as a protest against fascist rule on behalf of the German working-class. Historians still argue about the case; there is disagreement about whether he acted alone and some historians believe that the fire may have been started by the Nazis themselves as a pretext for bringing in tough laws against political opponents. Whatever the truth they certainly used the fire to further their political ends.

On the next day President Hindenburg was persuaded by Hitler to sign a decree which severely restricted civil liberties including giving the government the right to ban certain publications. Hitler announced that the fire was the beginning of an attempted Communist takeover and there followed mass arrests of leading Communists across Germany. In the elections held a week after the fire in a frenzied anti-Communist atmosphere, the Nazis achieved an effective majority in the Reichstag for the first time.

The building itself was unusable after the fire. The newly elected Reichstag met not far away in the Krolloper (The Kroll Opera House) which became the substitute home of the German Parliament until the end of the Third Reich. The deputies meeting there quickly passed the Enabling Act which handed virtually unlimited power to Hitler. The Reichstag, thereafter, was merely a puppet legislature with no real power which met periodically into the war years until April 1942.

The Kroll Opera House, which had been built in 1844, was severely damaged in an Allied bombing raid on 22 November 1943, further damaged during the Red Army's assault on the Reichstag in April 1945 and finally demolished in 1956. Today the area is grassed.

The Reichstag building, which had been built in 1894, lay in ruins at the end of the Second World War. Soviet troops famously planted the red flag on its roof to symbolise the capture of Berlin but the building had not by then been used for over a decade and was not to be used meaningfully again for a further four decades.

The building fell in the Western half of Berlin but was very close to the Wall. In the 1960s there was a partial renovation and it was occasionally used for one-off events. The two Germanys, however, each had their own

After the fire in 1933 rendered the building unusable, the Reichstag met at the nearby Kroll Opera House, here in session in 1941 (Bundesarchiv, Schwan)

The Kroll Opera House was demolished after extensive bomb damage in 1945 (Bundesarchiv, Otto Donath)

Allied bomb damage at the Reichstag towards the end of the war in early 1945 (Sergeant Hewitt, British Army Film and Photography Unit)

parliaments – East Germany's meeting in East Berlin and West Germany's in Bonn.

German reunification was declared by Chancellor Helmut Kohl on 3 November 1990 in the Reichstag building but there was a long debate about whether to make Berlin once again the capital of the reunited country. The vote to do so in June 1991 was won by just eighteen votes – 338 to 320. The building was redesigned by the British architect Sir Norman Foster and the Bundestag met in the Reichstag for the first time in 1999. The glass cupola which is the best-known feature of the new design is one of the most visited tourist attractions in Germany.

The Reichstag, restored as the seat of the German Parliament after reunification in 1990, is now a major tourist destination (Colin Philpott)

SUMMARY

I draw three main conclusions about the legacy of this group of Nazi locations – locations associated with terror and the enforcement of Nazi rule in Germany particularly in the years from 1933 to 1939.

Pragmatism is again a primarily important factor. With the benefit of hindsight, the decision to use the very barracks at Dachau where prisoners had been incarcerated, tortured, and, in many cases, allowed to die, to house refugees and the homeless after the war seems cruel. Given the deprivations of post-war Germany with much of the country lying in ruins, however, it probably made sense. The reuse of the NS-Ordensburgen complexes for military training and the Air Ministry as post-war government buildings was also based on pragmatic reasons although easier because the buildings were not associated with terror.

Secondly, the story of how Dachau was first turned into a memorial site in the 1960s demonstrates the driving role played by survivors and families of victims of Nazi terror in establishing the idea of memorialising such sites. It was only later that the political establishment provided its supportive backing.

Thirdly, although the permanent exhibition 'Topography of Terror' was only opened on the site of the Gestapo Headquarters in 2010, the temporary exhibition established there in 1987 was one of the first to be established at so-called 'perpetrator sites'. This perhaps reflects the special need felt in the German capital to acknowledge the shame of the Nazi period.

CHAPTER FOUR

Showing Off to the World
(Vorführung auf der Weltbühne)

PREAMBLE

As the 1930s wore on, the Nazi leadership grew in confidence and, buttressed by propaganda, persuasion and terror, their hold over Germany strengthened. They began to flex their military muscles and their expanding international ambitions became clearer. Alongside rearmament and a variety of actions designed to exert Germany's diplomatic rights they also sought to project Nazism onto the international stage mixing military threat with apparently peaceful showmanship.

Olympic Stadium Berlin with Olympic and Nazi flags flying for the opening ceremony on 1 August 1936 (Bundesarchiv, A.Frankel)

The Olympic Games of 1936, awarded before the Nazis came to power, provided a perfect opportunity to present a vision of the new Germany to the international community. The Winter Games, held in the Bavarian resorts of Garmisch and Partenkirchen, were a relatively modest taster for the Summer Games which took place in grand new facilities in Berlin.

The World's Fair in Paris the following year provided another opportunity for grandstanding on the international stage. International posturing was also evident in the building of new airports in Germany's two leading cities with Berlin's Tempelhof and Munich's Riem airports becoming its signature gateways.

A much more modest building associated with this phase of the Nazi era deserves a mention because, despite its relative lack of substance, the Führerbau in Munich, Hitler's base for entertaining in Bavaria, played host to one of the most important diplomatic meetings of the twentieth-century – here the British Prime Minister, Neville Chamberlain, put his name to the notorious and ultimately worthless Munich agreement.

GARMISCH-PARTENKIRCHEN WINTER OLYMPIC SITES, BAVARIA

The role of the 1936 Olympics in the history of the Third Reich bears some similarity to that of the German autobahn network. Like the motorways, the Olympics predated the Nazis. The 1936 Games had been awarded to Germany after a vote at the International Olympic Committee in 1931. Like the idea of a network of motorways, Hitler was initially sceptical about the value of the Olympics. In power, however, the Nazi leadership's view changed because Joseph Goebbels recognised the enormous propaganda potential which the Games offered. Hitler became persuaded to adopt the Olympics and turn them into a massive state-sponsored project to project the new Germany onto the international stage.

Early in February 1936, just days before the Winter Games were due to start, the Nazis' hopes of international recognition were threatened by a factor beyond their control – relatively warm winter temperatures in the Bavarian mountains. Luckily for the organisers, it snowed heavily immediately before the Games started on 6 February and Hitler arrived to open the Games amid rapturous cheers and heavy snowfall.

Potential international criticism of their racial policies was another reason for nervousness among the Nazi leadership prior to the opening of the Winter Games. By 1936 their persecution of Jews was well underway and there was little attempt to disguise it with anti-Semitic signs and slogans commonplace in most German towns and cities including in the twin-towns of Garmisch and Partenkirchen. The Germans knew that some countries, notably the United States, were already concerned about their anti-Jewish

View of the main skiing area at the 1936 Winter Olympics at Garmisch-Partenkirchen (Unknown)

Hitler watching the events at the Winter Olympics, Garmisch-Partenkirchen, February 1936 (Bundesarchiv, Willy Rehor)

Hitler saluting at the Winter Olympic Games, Garmisch-Partenkircken, February 1936 (Bundesarchiv, Heinrich Hoffman)

Hitler with Rudolf Hess and others at the opening of the Winter Olympics at Garmisch-Partenkirchen, February 1936 (Bundesarchiv, unknown)

policies and talk of boycotting the Games was in the air – something they were determined to prevent.

Karl Ritter von Halt, the chair of the German Olympic Organising Committee of the Winter Games, was fearful that any anti-Jewish sentiment or violence in Garmisch-Partenkirchen would not only tarnish the Winter Games but also the main event – the Summer Games in Berlin six months later. He complained to the Nazi leadership and a swift clean-up and clampdown followed. Signs and slogans were removed and orders went out to Nazi storm troopers and others to lay off anti-Jewish violence for the duration of the Games.

Sonja Henie – triple gold-medallist figure skater from Norway at the 1936 Winter Olympics – her success at the Games launched a Hollywood career (Bundesarchiv, unknown)

The Garmisch-Partenkirchen stadium looks little changed from 1936 (Unknown)

Garmisch-Partenkirchen was something of a 'forced marriage' of two quite distinct towns nestling below Germany's highest mountain, the Zugspitze. Hitler forced an amalgamation of the two towns as part of the preparation for the Games. The events lasted from 6-16 February and involved downhill Alpine skiing for the first time as well as the traditional Nordic winter sports. Twenty-eight nations took part in seventeen events and Norway won most medals including eight golds, three of them won by the figure skater Sonja Henie whose exploits at Garmisch were to launch a Hollywood film career. Henie, whose Nazi sympathies and admiration for Hitler were barely disguised, remains one of the most successful skaters of all time.

Many of the facilities built for the 1936 Winter Games still exist and Garmisch-Partenkirchen remains a leading skiing resort and winter sports venue. The most notable locations were the Ice Stadium built in Garmisch and the Ski Stadium in Partenkirchen. The Ski Stadium was built to hold 100,000 spectators and its central feature was the Olympiahaus containing a restaurant and VIP viewing platform from where Hitler and other dignitaries viewed the sporting action. The ski jump has been revamped twice since 1936 – in the 1950s and in 2007 but the overall feel of the resort is little changed since the Third Reich era.

The Winter Olympics in 1936 launched Garmisch-Partenkirchen's future as a major winter sports venue and tourist destination, a role which has since brought it considerable prosperity. The ambiguities in the attitude of the town and its people to these Nazi legacies three-quarters of a century later were highlighted when Garmisch-Partenkirchen bid in 2011 with Munich to host the 2018 Winter Olympics. The bid was unsuccessful but, during the bidding process, the town was naturally keen to emphasise the sporting heritage of 1936 rather than its political legacy.

The literature surrounding the 2011 bid and the commemorative brochure produced on the sixtieth anniversary of the Games give maximum emphasis to the sport with little or no reference to the role the 1936 Games played in Nazi propaganda. Despite some discussion about a museum or exhibition in the town to tell the full story of the Games there has been no follow-up. After tourist complaints in 2006 that the town's football stadium was still named after the organiser of the 1936 Games, the committed Nazi Karl Ritter von Halt, it was quietly renamed. Overall there seems to be rather less enthusiasm for acknowledging Garmisch-Partenkirchen's role in the Nazi story than is found in many other German towns and cities.

Garmisch-Partenkirchen is still a thriving winter sports resort today and many of the facilities built in 1936 are still in use (Martin Fisch)

Arguments have been made that the survival, and indeed development, of the sporting facilities bequeathed by the 1936 Winter Olympics are tainted by association with the Nazis. The towns have derived great benefit from the Nazi investment in the games but the locations were not scenes of terror and to have destroyed the sites and the excellent sporting facilities would surely have been an act of unnecessary vandalism.

OLYMPIC STADIUM, BERLIN

The Olympic Stadium in Berlin highlights, even more than Garmisch-Partenkirchen, the dilemma associated with attitudes to the architecture of the Third Reich. Leaving from the U-bahn station and walking up the wide, gently-sloping piazza which leads to the stadium, there are two contrasting narratives on display.

The first is that this patch of land in the western suburbs of Berlin will forever be associated with one of the most ostentatious propaganda exercises undertaken by any twentieth-century regime. An international event, conceived as a vehicle for celebrating sporting excellence and fostering harmony between countries, was hijacked in the most cynical way by racist ideologues presenting a falsely serene view of their regime to the world. This view makes it difficult, if not impossible, to separate the

View of the Olympic Stadium, Berlin from the air during the 1936 Summer Olympic Games (Bundesarchiv, Heinrich Hoffman)

The distinctive 1930s architecture of the Olympic Stadium, Berlin – the pillars surrounding the stadium (Colin Philpott)

architecture from the political motivation. The stadium and the other associated structures are irredeemably grim and foreboding. It is almost as though the walls have trapped within them the cheers of 100,000 people welcoming Hitler with Nazi salutes. Newsreel images of swastikas fluttering in the wind alongside the Olympic flag still seem to haunt the place.

The alternative view is that the Berlin Olympic Stadium is a superb example of 1930s architecture. Perhaps its most striking feature is the way it is deliberately sunk into the ground with the surface of the sporting arena 12m below ground level. The effect is to make it look smaller from the outside. Once inside the stadium itself the volume and scale of the arena below ground level become apparent. The neo-classical concrete symmetry of the stadium is both compelling and impressive and makes this an appropriate building for an event of truly international significance.

Hitler's attempts to turn the eleventh modern Olympiad into an international showcase were not wholly successful. The Nazi script was threefold – meticulous choreography, faultless organisation and Aryan sporting superiority. The first two objectives may have been achieved but the third was not. Several decidedly non-Aryan competitors, most notably the black American runner and long-jumper, Jesse Owens, ignored the script and won medals under the noses of the Nazi leadership.

With this interpretation not only is the Berlin Olympic Stadium great architecture but the event for which it was built turned out to be, despite the intentions of the Nazi propagandists, an international sporting spectacle in the true tradition of the Olympics. The memories embodied in the stadium are therefore as much those of international sporting prowess as of Nazi propaganda. This is the legacy that is represented by the sites associated with the 1936 Berlin Olympics the honours board of which remains to commemorate achievements of Owens and others.

The Nazi regime unquestionably grabbed the Olympic opportunity presented serendipitously to them when they came to power with enormous enthusiasm. Prior to 1933 the German Olympic Organising Committee had been developing plans for the facilities necessary to stage the Games. The original proposal was to rebuild the 64,000 capacity Deutsches Stadion which had been opened in 1913 in the middle of the Grunewald Racecourse. Originally intended to stage the 1916 Olympics, awarded to Berlin but cancelled because of the First World War, that stadium had mainly been used for football during the 1920s and early 1930s.

Once he had embraced the propaganda possibilities offered by the Olympics, Hitler's plans became more ambitious and he demanded a larger, grander stadium. Werner March, the original architect, was retained but

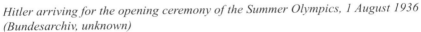

Hitler arriving for the opening ceremony of the Summer Olympics, 1 August 1936 (Bundesarchiv, unknown)

commissioned to think big. The stadium was the centrepiece of an Olympic complex which also included an open-air amphitheatre, the Maifeld which could hold 250,000, the Haus der Deutschen Sport and a number of other venues. No resources were spared and the full force of the German state supported the project to ensure preparation of an impressive stage for the Games.

Saturday 1 August 1936 represents perhaps the apogee of Hitler and the Nazis' peacetime straddling of the national and international stages. Hitler, now secure in power, arrived in the Olympic Stadium that afternoon to tumultuous cheers and Nazi salutes. With both the apparent plaudits of his people and international acceptance, however reluctant, he could bask in a glorious moment. As the teams of the competing nations streamed past the Führer during the opening ceremony some foreign competitors even made the Nazi salute.

Earlier controversies, however, had created doubt that the opening ceremony would ever take place. Concern had been expressed from various quarters around the world, almost from the moment that Hitler took power in early 1933, that the 1931 award had become a poisoned chalice. The obvious persecution of Jews was soon apparent and gave rise to talk of boycotts both by countries and by individuals. The Germans had given assurances that Jewish athletes would be allowed to compete in their team although eventually only one Jewish competitor, the fencer Helene Mayer, was selected to represent the home nation.

Such protests, however, faded – particularly after the United States Olympic Committee decided to participate. Some individuals from a number of countries refused to attend but they were few and far between. Controversy has persisted ever since about the attitude of the International Olympic Committee towards the Berlin Games. Should they have taken a tougher stand against Germany or even considered moving the Games elsewhere? With the benefit of hindsight, it wouldn't be difficult to put up an argument that they should have done but, in the appeasement fuelled political atmosphere of the time, the decision was unsurprising. Furthermore there was the conviction that Germany would organise the Games very well.

For two weeks in August 1936, the world's attention was on Berlin and the Germans put on a show. The organisation was meticulous and everything pretty much went like clockwork. Facilities were ready on time and the administration was excellent. The Games were the first to be televised to twenty or more public viewing screens in Berlin and Potsdam. The anti-Jewish slogans were removed and the regime assumed a deceptively benign face for the world; its excesses were largely put on hold for the duration of the Games.

Competitors from a number of nations made Nazi salutes on the podium at the 1936 Berlin Olympics (Bundesarchiv, Stempka)

Forty-nine nations took part in 129 events involving nineteen different sports. Germany won the largest medals tally (eighty-nine with thirty-three golds) but Jesse Owens won four golds in the 100m, 200m, long jump and the 4x100m relay. Hitler famously snubbed him despite these achievements.

Amid the destruction of Berlin in the final weeks of the war in the spring of 1945 the Olympic Stadium remained largely unscathed. Many of the other Olympic buildings were damaged but the stadium stood like a beacon amid the ruins of the city – one of the largest buildings to survive the Battle of Berlin. In the post-war political arrangements the stadium fell in the British sector of Berlin but the Olympic village was under Russian control. The Reichsportsfeld was used as the headquarters of the British military forces in Berlin. The Olympic Stadium itself became home of Hertha Berlin Football Club when the West German Bundesliga was formed in 1963. It was given protected historical monument status in 1966 and refurbished for the 1974 World Cup; partial roofing was constructed and three matches were hosted there.

Serious discussion took place after German reunification over the possibility of demolishing the Stadium which needed major refurbishment if it was to become the main national stadium of the new Germany – a factor in this debate being its association with the Nazi era. On 1 December 1998, however, the Berlin Senate approved a 242 million Euros redevelopment in preparation for what proved to be a successful bid to host the 2006 World Cup. Six matches including the final took place there.

Jesse Owens, who won four gold medals at the Berlin Olympics, confounding Nazi theories of Aryan superiority (Olympic Games Official record, unknown)

Since then the Olympic Stadium has hosted world-class sporting events including the 2009 World Athletic Championships when Usain Bolt established new world records, still standing in 2015, at both the 100m and 200m distances. The stadium, which hosts concerts and other events and remains the home of Hertha Berlin FC, hosted the UEFA Champions League Final in June 2015.

Interior of the Berlin Olympic Stadium after its refurbishment for the 2006 football World Cup (Colin Philpott)

Of the other Olympic structures, the Deutschlandhalle, which hosted boxing, weightlifting and wrestling, was finally demolished in 2011 despite its historical monument status. It had been rebuilt after the war as a multi-purpose sports and entertainment venue but by the twenty-first century was outshone by other and newer Berlin venues. A purpose-built ice arena now stands on the site. The Maifeld is now a park. The swimming pool remains and is used occasionally. The Dietrich-Eckart Open Air Theatre is also still in use (see Chapter Two – Thingstätten). In 1984 a road near the stadium was renamed Jesse-Owens-Allee.

The most forlorn remains of the 1936 Olympics are a few miles away from the stadium at the site of the Olympic village. This was part of the Soviet zone of occupation and was used as an interrogation centre by the KGB. Since the Soviet departure in the 1980s it has remained a ruin. It can be visited but the only room that has been restored and preserved is the one occupied by Jesse Owens during the Games. Plans were announced in 2015 to redevelop the area for housing but it remains a sad monument to the genuine mixing of competitors that took place there in 1936 in defiance of the racist ideology of the hosts.

Berlin would of course welcome the opportunity to stage another Olympics free of the inevitable associations with the politics of 1936. In

Rudolf Hess at the Olympic Village several miles from the main Olympic site (Bundesarchiv, Heinrich Hoffman)

Remains of the dining room at the Olympic Village which is still largely derelict eighty years after the Games took place (Voice of America, unknown)

Remains of the Olympic Village swimming pool – there are hopes of a restoration of the site as a housing development (N.Lange)

Berlin's Olympic Stadium has hosted many major sporting and cultural events since the Nazi era (Colin Philpott)

March 2015, however, the city lost out to Hamburg to be the nominated German bidder for the 2024 Games and so must await its turn.

Christopher Hilton, in his study of the 1936 Games *'Hitler's Olympics'* says that the stadium and the other Olympic remains from 1936 retain a studious grandeur. 'They still fulfil their original, cumulative purpose; to take your breath away.' He speculates as to why this is the case 'Perhaps it has to do with the perfect proportions; perhaps the imposing stonework; perhaps the knowledge that in August 1936 the world of sport had seen nothing to equal it; perhaps because here a poor black American sharecropper's son brought the potential of the human body to an astonishing, immortal climax. Or perhaps because with hindsight we know what cataclysmic events came afterwards. Or maybe because Hitler built it and strode into it at a time when he truly stood at the centre of the world.'

This area of Berlin will forever be remembered for the Hitler Games but it was also the site of the achievements of Jesse Owens and many others at those Games. Many other great sporting and cultural events have been staged since 1936 at this site which has been remodelled to produce one of the most awe-inspiring stadiums in the world. Nazi architecture is not necessarily bad architecture just because it is Nazi architecture. It has been rightly preserved and reinvented.

THE GERMAN PAVILION AT THE WORLD'S FAIR, PARIS.

Most of the locations featured in this study are in Germany, or in what was Germany at the time of the Third Reich, but this structure at the heart of the French capital deserves a mention.

Between May to November 1937 the World's Fair took place in the centre of Paris. The Exposition Internationale des Arts et Techniques dans la Vie Moderne (The International Exhibition of Arts and Technology in Modern Life) was designed to show off contemporary scientific and technological achievement with pavilions devoted to then new technologies like cinema, radio and aviation.

Forty-four participating nations each had a pavilion to show off their attainments. Germany and the Soviet Union were, almost certainly by accident rather than design, allocated prime sites opposite each other across the Seine from the Eiffel Tower. At first, as with other projects like the Olympics, Hitler was not enthusiastic about the World's Fair but was persuaded by his chief architect, Albert Speer, of the importance of Germany being seen on this international stage.

Apocryphally, Speer found a copy of the design of the planned Russian pavilion when visiting the Paris site some months before the opening and decided to ensure the German pavilion would be taller than its Soviet rival. Whether true or not, the German pavilion indeed towered above the Soviet

The German Pavilion at the World's Fair, Paris, 1937 designed by Albert Speer (unknown)

one. It was made of steel with a Bavarian marble surface topped by a giant German eagle. To ensure that it was built on time, and as Speer exactly required, more than 1,000 German workers were transported to Paris for its completion.

The pavilion was dismantled after the exhibition and the fate of its materials remains a mystery.

BERLIN TEMPELHOF AND MUNICH RIEM AIRPORTS
Two airports in Germany's two leading cities, both created as monuments to Nazism and both now closed to air traffic, are further examples of the grandiose architectural ambitions of the Third Reich. They are best known for events after the Nazi era – Tempelhof for the Berlin Airlift of 1948 and

Munich-Riem for the 1958 air crash which cost the lives of many of the Manchester United football team and others. Although no longer airports, they both survive in the twenty-first century with new uses but with the Nazi connection ever-present.

The former Tempelhof Airport, south of the centre of Berlin, is yet another pre-existing site which was appropriated by the Nazis after their assumption of power for propaganda and practical reasons. Tempelhof was an airfield in the early years of flying before the First World War and the great aviation pioneer Orville Wright was one of the first to land there. The first operational terminal building dated from 1927 but, after 1933, Albert Speer commissioned Ernst Sagebiel to redesign Tempelhof in a style befitting the capital of the Third Reich.

Like many other Nazi projects, it was conceived on a monumental scale. The outcome was something far bigger than necessary for the actual needs of a 1930s airport. Its main feature is the quadrant-shaped terminal building over 1km long with lofty arrivals and departure halls. Building began in

Planes on the tarmac at Berlin Tempelhof, 1948 around the time of the Berlin Airlift (US Air Force)

Berlin Tempelhof Airport Main Buildings which remain since the closure of the airport in 2008 (Alan Ford)

1936 and continued into the early years of the war when the airport was one of the largest buildings in the world. Relative proximity to the city centre and the building of its own U-bahn station helped its development.

In the latter half of the 1930s, as commercial aviation grew in popularity, Tempelhof became one of the busiest airports in the world and compared with Paris-Le Bourget and London Croydon as the glamorous hubs of a new form of transport only available to the wealthy. At its peak Tempelhof received over 100 flights daily using the old terminal building while the new one was under construction – and that remained unfinished during the Third Reich.

Part of Tempelhof was built on the site of one of the earliest Nazi concentration camps, Columbia, which had opened in 1933 but which was closed three years later to make way for the airport.

During the Second World War, Tempelhof was used as a base for assembling Junkers Stuka dive bombers although it was not used as a military airfield. The Russians captured the airport during the Battle of Berlin in the last days of April 1945 and that July, under the terms of the Potsdam Agreement, the airport became part of the American occupation zone from where commercial flying resumed in February 1946.

Tempelhof's biggest claim to fame began in June 1948. The western-controlled sectors of Berlin were surrounded by the Soviet-controlled sector of Germany. Land routes between West Berlin and West Germany had been agreed but, as tensions mounted between the West and the Soviet Union, these were blocked by the Russians. West Berlin could only remain connected to the West by the three air corridors which were part of the 1945 agreement. For almost a year the Western Allies organised a continuous stream of aircraft bringing vital supplies into West Berlin via Tempelhof before the Russians called off the land blockade in May 1949.

From the 1950s onwards Tempelhof developed as a major commercial airport peaking in the early 1970s with over five million passengers a year. It also retained a military role until the fall of the Berlin Wall led to the withdrawal of American forces in 1994.

By the 1990s Tempelhof's position as Berlin's leading airport was already weakening. Some airlines had transferred to Berlin Tegel and, by the mid-nineties, Tempelhof's main traffic was smaller commuter flights. In 1996 plans were announced to create a single unified airport for Berlin based next to Schönefeld Airport; these required the closure of first

Interior of main hall at Berlin Tempelhof – visitors can tour the building and see this remnant of Nazi architecture (Alan Ford)

Berliners enjoying Tempelhofer Freiheit Park which has been created as a public park on the site of the former airport (Berlin Tempelhofer Freiheit, Nic Simanek)

Tempelhof and then Tegel airports. A non-binding referendum in Berlin failed to stop the closure and the last flights left Tempelhof at the end of October 2008.

Tempelhof has since enjoyed a new lease of life. It is now a massive urban park known as Tempelhofer Freiheit, bigger than New York's Central Park, and crowds flock there daily to enjoy Berlin's 'urban lung'. Concerts and sports events are staged and tours can be taken around the old preserved terminal buildings. The historical legacy of Tempelhof is also marked by a memorial to those who suffered and died at the Columbia Concentration Camp. The main U-bahn station serving the area was renamed to commemorate the Berlin Airlift – it is now called Platz der Luftbrücke. In 2014 a plan to build a large housing development on part of the site was defeated in a referendum. Berliners have taken Tempelhof to their hearts. Meanwhile, Berlin's new airport is beset by delays and problems and not due to open until 2017. In 2015 both Tegel and Schönefeld airports remain in use.

Munich-Riem was also a product of the Third Reich designed as a prestigious gateway to the Bavarian capital. Work started in 1936 and the airport opened in 1939. Hitler flew in to Munich-Riem in November 1939 as one of the first passengers to use the airport. It replaced Munich's previous airport at Oberwiesenfeld – an area nearer the city centre which

Remaining terminal building from Munich-Riem Airport which has been preserved as part of the redevelopment of the site since its closure as an airport (Florian Schutz)

One small section of the runway at Munich-Riem Airport can still be seen (Pahu)

New conference and events centre development of Messestadt Riem on the site of Munich-Riem Airport (Unknown)

later became the site for the 1972 Olympics. Immediately it was opened, Munich-Riem was pressed into service for military purposes although civilian flights continued through much of the war.

On 9 April 1945 an Allied air raid virtually destroyed the airport but it was rebuilt and reopened in 1948 as a commercial airport. Its traffic grew steadily and there were various improvements over the years. As early as the 1960s, however, Munich recognised that it would eventually need a new airport as expansion at Riem would involve sacrificing nearby communities. Another thirty years elapsed before, in May 1992, Riem closed and was replaced by the new Munich Franz Josef-Strauss Airport.

In the early years after its closure Munich-Riem Airport was the scene of a lively alternative music scene hosting concerts and raves. The area has now been redeveloped as Messestadt Riem, a convention centre with associated housing and other developments. The control tower and terminal building of the old airport are preserved as historical monuments.

Munich-Riem Airport is most associated with the events of 6 February 1958 when a charter plane returning the Manchester United football team from a European Cup tie in Belgrade crashed on take-off. Twenty-three people died including eight members of the team. The cause of the crash was eventually established as slush on the runway. There is a memorial to the crash victims at the airport site.

FÜHRERBAU BUILDING, MUNICH, BAVARIA

In the early hours of 30 September 1938, the leaders of Germany, France, Britain and Italy signed an agreement on the second floor of number 12, Arcisstrasse, north of the centre of Munich. Two of the signatories believed that this culmination of several weeks of shuttle diplomacy would prevent another war. The meeting in Munich was the third visit to Germany in a fortnight by the British Prime Minister, Neville Chamberlain, as he vainly sought to prevent conflict.

Exterior of the Führerbau building, Munich, 1938 where Hitler entertained guests when in the Bavarian capital (Bundesarchiv, unknown)

Neville Chamberlain, the French leader Edouard Daladier, Adolf Hitler, Benito Mussolini and the Italian Minister of Foreign Affairs Galeazzo Ciano in the Führerbau, September 1938 (Bundesarchiv, unknown)

Britain and France agreed to Hitler's demands, backed by the Italian leader Mussolini, for the so-called Sudetenland (areas of Czechoslovakia with significant German speaking populations) to be ceded to Germany. Chamberlain believed that the agreement would appease Hitler and be the limit of his territorial ambitions – a belief that proved to be very wrong. The Czech government wasn't invited to Munich and saw the agreement as a betrayal by Britain and France. Within a year Chamberlain's hopes, and those of the French, had been dashed. Hitler ignored the terms of the deal and later invaded the whole of Czechoslovakia and, within a year, Poland; the world was at war again little more than twenty years after the war to end all wars had finished.

On his return to London after what became known as the Munich Agreement Neville Chamberlain claimed that he had secured 'peace in our time'.

When I dragged my family round the streets of Munich to find 12 Arcisstrasse some years ago, they wondered why we had bothered to seek out such an ordinary building. The very ordinariness of the place where such a momentous act of diplomacy took place, however, accounts for its fascination. Imagining those four men gathered together in a simple room less than a year before they would be at war feels painfully poignant.

Interior of what was Hitler's study at the Führerbau during the time of the Munich Agreement (Unknown)

At the time of the signature Arcisstrasse 12 was the Führerbau; it was designed by the architect Paul Troost and completed in 1934 as a building for entertaining by the Nazi leadership when in Munich. After the war the US occupation forces used it as a collecting place for the recovery of works of art looted by the Nazis. When it later reverted to the German authorities it became the home of the Hochschule für Musik und Theater (The University of Applied Sciences of Music and Theatre) and still performs that role.

There is, perhaps unsurprisingly, no plaque on the wall and no particular commemoration of the momentous events that took place in this building. However, since April 2015, the opening of the new NS-Documentation Centre around the corner on the site of the former Braun Haus (see Chapter One) has brought renewed attention to this area of Munich and its Nazi past. It is now possible to take a tour inside the building and to enter the room where the Munich Agreement was signed. It looks very much as it did on that fateful day more than three generations ago.

SUMMARY

The group of buildings and sites discussed in this chapter demonstrate perhaps above all others in this study the relative disconnect that now exists between the reasons for their construction during the Third Reich and their continued subsequent existence. The principal purpose of constructing all these buildings was to show off Nazi Germany – vast Olympic facilities, grand new airports, a pavilion at an international exhibition and a more modest but highly significant entertainment building for the Nazi leadership.

With the exception of the German Pavilion at the World's Fair, which was only ever intended to be temporary, the others remain and indeed are now enjoying new leases of life in many ways unrelated to their Nazi origins. Both the airports stopped being airports only because the demands of growing air traffic had made them unfit for purpose by the end of the twentieth century.

Most of the sites featured in this section are both fine and useful buildings and spaces. To have torn them down would have been hugely

The Führerbau today – like many Nazi-era buildings which have found a new use – as the Hochschule für Musik und Theater (Colin Philpott)

wasteful and a wanton attack on the country's architectural legacy despite their Nazi provenance.

Those relaxing in the parkland that once was Tempelhof Airport or watching a football match in the Olympic Stadium still talk about, and are aware of, the historic connection with the Nazis – and that link to 'dark history' may well be part of the reason for some visits seventy-five years later. None of these places, however, was directly associated with Nazi terror and all are also known for other reasons – the Berlin Airlift, the 2006 World Cup, the achievements of Jesse Owens. Their appropriate reinvention and adaptation allows us to feel at ease that they are still enjoyed today.

CHAPTER FIVE

Future Fantasies
(Zukunftsphantasien)

PREAMBLE

Nazi Germany built and destroyed much but also planned a great deal which never came to fruition. The most grandiloquent of these ambitions was the plan to rebuild Berlin as the capital of the world, renamed Germania (Welthauptstadt Germania), with new buildings on a scale dwarfing anything previously seen anywhere.

The architectural fantasies of Hitler and Speer extended far beyond Berlin including plans to rebuild the conquered Polish capital of Warsaw, plans for a series of Führerstädte across the Greater German Reich and even for a new city on the Norwegian coast.

The remains of the Nuremberg Congress Hall from above – much of the building is now used as a store for the Nuremberg Symphony Orchestra (Nico Hoffman)

Most of these ideas remained on the drawing board but evidence remains of some test sites built in various locations for buildings which never materialised and, most eerily of all, the half-built structure which would have been the largest indoor conference hall in the world.

WELTHAUPTSTADT GERMANIA, BERLIN

South of the centre of Berlin on Dudenstrasse, not far from the former Tempelhof Airport, is a tower standing almost 20m high which looks rather incongruous amid its modern surroundings. It was constructed in 1941 to test the load-bearing properties of the unstable ground on which Berlin is built. The objective was to check if the ground was strong enough to support a proposed triumphal arch. It was also a test for a range of other monumental buildings across Berlin as part of the remodelling of the German capital. The results of this experiment became irrelevant along with the plans themselves because the war delayed them before defeat ensured their cancellation.

Copious evidence of what the Nazis planned, nevertheless, remains. Many photographs exist of Hitler, Speer and other Nazi leaders standing proudly alongside models of how Berlin was to be transformed. With the benefit of hindsight the pictures can now be seen as impossible megalomaniac visions of deluded tyrants. Without doubt the Nazis were deadly serious – however hard it is to believe that these and other plans for

Hitler and Speer looking at plans for the vast remodelling of Berlin as 'Germania' in 1939 (Bundesarchiv, unknown)

Model of 'Welthauptstadt Germania' – the planned redevelopment of Berlin by the
Nazis as Capital of the Greater Reich (Bundesarchiv, unknown)

buildings and public spaces on such gargantuan scale could have been constructed.

The vision for Germania as Welthaupstadt (World Capital) of a triumphant Germany was part of Hitler's dream of world domination. It involved making Berlin a city to stand alongside and exceed other great capitals of the world including London, Paris and Rome. The central concept of these plans, developed by Speer before the outbreak of war, was that Berlin would be redesigned along two great axes running East-West and North-South.

The new North-South axis would have run from a point near the Brandenburg Gate south to a point not far from Tempelhof Airport. Land was obtained and some clearance took place to create this new road which would have been closed to normal traffic and assigned as a parade ground and route for military vehicles. The road would have been around 5km long, 120m wide and would have been flanked by new buildings. Partly constructed underground tunnels were to provide alternative routes for ordinary traffic.

The crowning glories of this vision were the proposed buildings at either end of the new road. At the northern end, near the Reichstag, there were plans for a 'People's Hall', or Volkshalle, 200m high and with a dome sixteen times larger than that of St. Peter's in Rome. It would have towered above Berlin's existing buildings including the Reichstag and the Brandenburg Gate. At the southern end was the proposed site for the Triumphal Arch modelled on the Arc de Triomphe in Paris but deliberately designed to surpass it in grandeur. The proposed arch would have stood 100m high and the Parisian landmark would have been able to fit underneath it.

The East-West axis was partly realised with the widening of what was then Charlottenburger Chaussee. Speer's overall vision for Germania did include some buildings which were finished including the Olympic Stadium (see Chapter Four) and the Reich Chancellery (see Chapter Eight) but, grand though these were, they were modest by comparison with the scale of those that remained architects' drawings.

Even compared with the public spaces and monumental buildings of other countries, particularly totalitarian ones, these proposed structures and spaces were seriously overbearing and on a scale out of all proportion to their surroundings. The message was twofold. Firstly, they were designed to demonstrate the power and scale of the Nazi state – with individual citizens of the Third Reich feeling very small inside public spaces designed to hold over 350,000 people. Secondly, these buildings would, in the minds of the Nazi leaders, give Germany a capital to rival other nations.

It is tempting to dismiss these unrealised architectural dreams as a slightly trivial postscript to the excesses of the Nazi regime but they

Schwerbelastungskörper (heavy load-bearing body) Tower which was constructed to test the ability of the Berlin ground to withstand the massive structures planned by Albert Speer for 'Welthaupstadt Germania' (Dieter Brugmann)

produced much suffering. Significant excavation and demolition work occurred much of which was done by forced labour from concentration camps. This was one of the key facts demonstrated in an exhibition about the Germania vision entitled 'Mythos Germania' and staged during 2015 in a Nazi bunker in the city.

Back in Dudenstrasse, that original test tower or Schwerbelastungskörper (heavy load-bearing body) is now a listed monument. Consideration was given to demolishing it after the war but it was too close to apartment blocks. Today its historical significance is marked through preserved status and the tower is open to tours.

FÜHRERSTADT LINZ

The Nazi desire to rebuild cities across the Greater German Reich to reflect the ambitions and values of the regime knew no bounds. In 1937 Hitler conferred special status on five cities which were to be fashioned to Nazi ideals. They were Berlin, Nuremberg, Munich, Hamburg and the city where Hitler spent his youth – Linz in Austria. These places were to acquire the title of Führerstadt and were to undergo massive urban transformation in line with the grandiose architectural visions of Hitler supported by Speer and other leading Third Reich architects.

More than thirty other cities were also identified as worthy of less ambitious reconstruction but it was the five key places that received most attention although very little was built in furtherance of these plans. Each of the five cities had a specific role – Berlin, as already discussed as Welthaupstadt, Nuremberg as 'City of the Reich Party Conventions', Hamburg as 'Capital of German Shipping', Munich as 'Capital of the Movement' and Linz as 'The City of the Führer's Youth' – 'Jugendstadt des Führers'.

Both Nuremberg and Munich's plans were partially realised. As discussed previously, the remodelling of the area around the Königsplatz in Munich created a Nazi centre in the city. The Nuremberg Rally Grounds, though never completed to their full designs, were substantially finished. In Hamburg there were similar grand plans designed by the architect Konstanty Gutschow but these never materialised because of the advent of the war.

The story of Hitler's ambitions for Linz is perhaps the most interesting. The city where the Führer had spent a significant part of his early life was the one to which he imagined he would retire. His special affection for the Austrian city on the banks of the Danube gave rise to its particular place in the architectural plans of the Third Reich. Hitler envisaged Linz's dramatic reconstruction and expansion to turn it into the 'German Budapest'. Among the new buildings planned were an Olympic Stadium, a Kraft durch Freude (Strength through Joy) hotel, new headquarters for the Wehrmacht, new municipal and Nazi party buildings, a giant suspension bridge linking the banks of the Danube, a Führermuseum and a crypt where Hitler, having enjoyed a long and lengthy retirement in Linz, was to be buried.

Model of the planned redevelopment of the Austrian city of Linz on the banks of the Danube as Führerstadt Linz (Linz Kultur, unknown)

None of this happened although much time and effort was devoted to its planning and art was assembled from all over Europe, much of it stolen, as the first stage of a collection for the museum. Hitler envisaged this as a rival to the Louvre in Paris, the Uffizi in Florence or the Hermitage in St. Petersburg. Even in 1945, with the war clearly lost, Hitler was still giving orders for assembling art treasures ready for display in his favourite Austrian city.

PABST PLAN, WARSAW, POLAND AND NORDSTERN, NORWAY

The Nazis' grand architectural designs for reshaping cities were not confined within the borders of the Reich but extended well into captured territories across Europe.

Their scheme for the Polish capital of Warsaw was far more dramatic and brutal than the most ambitious plans for any German City. Even before

Map showing the so-called Pabst Plan for the rebuilding of Warsaw (Hubert Gross and Otto Nurnberger)

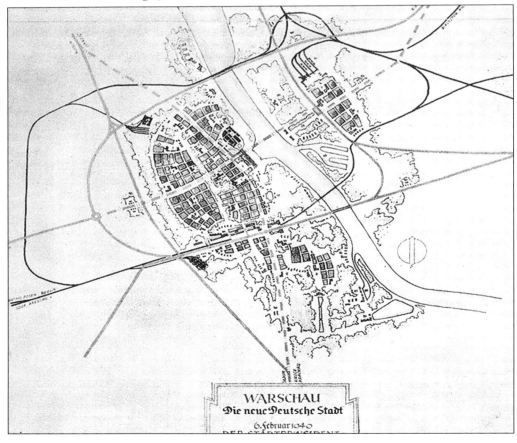

WARSCHAU
Die neue Deutsche Stadt
6. Februar 1940

The Warsaw Ghetto Uprising, 1943 – an estimated 300,000 people died in the ghetto during its three years (Unknown)

they invaded Poland in September 1939, the Nazis planned to destroy Warsaw almost completely and replace it with a much smaller 'German' city. The so-called Pabst Plan was named after Friedrich Pabst, the Nazi 'Chief Architect for Warsaw', although more than one plan was made during the years between the invasion of Poland and the collapse of the Third Reich.

In essence the various plans had one objective – the obliteration of the ancient city of Warsaw including most of its historic buildings. The new city, which was to house the German elite ruling the occupied Polish territories, would be only about a twentieth of the size of the existing city. Only a small proportion of the existing buildings, in the old town and on the riverbank, would be preserved. The new city would have a much smaller population – around 130,000 compared with the one and a half million people living in pre-war Warsaw. It would be comprised of 'ethnically pure' Germans with a forced labour settlement of non-Germans on the opposite bank of the Vistula River. These plans were inextricably linked with the Nazis' ideas of racial superiority and involved the forced removal of Jews from large parts of the city to a 'Jewish quarter' and ultimately their total removal from Warsaw.

The destructive elements of this plan were dramatically realised but the rebuilding was not. Ten per cent of Warsaw is estimated to have been destroyed in the initial 1939 invasion. This was used as a pretext by the occupiers for further destruction in the name of clearing the city to prepare for rebuilding. The only part of the new Warsaw that was ever built was the infamous 'Warsaw Ghetto'. In the autumn of 1940 the Germans forcibly removed Jews from across the city and beyond into a small area of northern Warsaw. Living conditions were appalling with an estimated 400,000 people living in an area little more than three square kilometres. Deportations to extermination camps became normal and, in early 1943, an uprising in the ghetto resulted in yet more brutal repression and culminated in its virtual destruction by the Germans. An estimated 300,000 people died in the Warsaw Ghetto during its three years.

Warsaw's agony was not to end there. In 1944 Hitler ordered the total destruction of the city and special German units were sent there to raze it to

Warsaw after its destruction, 1945 – an estimated eighty per cent of the city's buildings had been destroyed by the end of the Second World War (M.Swierczynski)

Trondheim, site of the proposed Nordstern city, Norway, 1942 – more than 50,000 homes were planned for this new settlement (Bundesarchiv, unknown)

the ground. Warsaw was to become nothing but a transit station for the German Wehrmacht. By the end of the war, an estimated eighty per cent of Warsaw's buildings had been destroyed. Astonishingly, the city has been substantially rebuilt since 1950.

Hitler's idea for a new naval base and city on the Norwegian coast was peaceful by comparison with his destruction of Warsaw but they were part of the same thrust – to establish German 'colonies' in occupied territories to reinforce the power of the Third Reich in countries it had conquered.

The motivation for building a substantial new city in the bay which included Trondheim in Norway was strategic. In order to have a better chance of dominating the North Atlantic, Germany needed a more northerly base for its warships. Refitting and repairing naval ships in Norway, rather than their forced return to German ports, would gain an advantage in naval battles with Britain.

The plan to create a new base and accompanying city about 15km south of Trondheim was officially adopted by Hitler in 1941 and was dubbed 'Nordstern' or North Star. A city with 250,000 inhabitants was planned alongside the new naval base which would include an underground submarine base hewn out of the cliff face. More than 50,000 homes were planned for the new city which would also have a museum and autobahn links to Trondheim and beyond. Hitler appointed Albert Speer to mastermind the project and he claimed it would become the 'Singapore of the German Empire'.

Work started in 1943 with the first excavations of the site, the building of an airstrip and the establishment of a prisoner of war camp designed to provide labour for the project. In 1944 the scheme was abandoned and the remains of the excavations can still be seen in the area.

Hitler retained a model of the proposed base and new city in his chancellery in Berlin. As he increasingly lost his comprehension of the reality of a defeat he took refuge in his architectural dreams right to the last and was seen poring over plans and models for Nordstern, Führerstadt Linz and elsewhere even a few weeks before his death.

DEUTSCHES STADION, ACHTEL, BAVARIA
Of all the sites in Germany associated with the Nazis, the partially obscured ruins to be found deep in the woods near the small Bavarian town of Achtel, about 40km from Nuremberg, are among the most remarkable. A series of concrete pillars buried in a hillside now covered in trees is all that remains of one of the most eye-watering architectural schemes ever conceived by the Nazis.

Model of the proposed 400,000 capacity Deutsches Stadion at Nuremberg, 1938 (NS-Reichsparteitagsgelände Dokumentationszentrum, Unknown)

Hitler, Speer and others visiting the test site for the Deutsches Stadion at Achtel in Bavaria, 1938 (Bundesarchiv, Unknown)

From 1937 until the outbreak of war in 1939, labourers toiled away on this Bavarian hillside as part of the project to build what would have been, by some measure, the largest stadium in the world and, had Hitler had his way, the venue for all future Olympic Games.

This site was not, however, the actual location of the proposed stadium. It was a prototype where the engineering and aesthetics and the sight lines of the giant stadium could be tested before full construction of the Deutsches Stadion went ahead on the Nuremberg Rally Grounds.

Hitler's vision was a stadium modelled on the stadia of ancient Greece but which could accommodate 400,000 people. It would have been built on the southern end of the Party Rally Grounds on the outskirts of Nuremberg. Its dimensions would have been breath-taking – 800m long by 450m wide and with its main façade about 90m high. The 1940 Olympic Games were due to be held in Tokyo but Hitler's view was that all subsequent Olympics would be staged in Germany in this massive new stadium. Excavations began there in 1938 but construction never started. After the war, the site was filled in and is now a lake.

Work on the test site at Achtel continued longer. It was chosen because the hillside had the same gradient as the proposed Deutsches Stadion and also because it was relatively remote and work on the experiment could be carried on in comparative secrecy. 400 workers built the concrete bases and

Remains of the test site for the Deutsches Stadion deep in woodland at Achtel (M.Klaus)

wooden terracing on the hillside to the same scale as the plan. About one tenth of the planned stadium was built on the hillside at Achtel. Hitler, Speer and other leading Nazis visited it more than once to inspect progress.

Like so many of the Nazis' grand schemes work stopped when the war started. At the end of the war, the test stadium was dismantled and its wood used to rebuild the village of Achtel which had been severely damaged in heavy fighting as the Americans advanced over the area. The concrete supports remained on the hillside but were gradually submerged as tree cover increased.

For several decades the site was ignored by local people keen to forget this particular association with the Nazi period. The hillside has now been partially cleared and the concrete remains have historic monument status; accordingly, seventy-five years on, the haunting remains of this monumental plan can be seen. It is difficult not to feel a grudging admiration for the ambition of the plan and the lengths to which Speer went to bring it to fruition by building a life-size test in semi-secrecy on a remote hillside. The concrete remains, at least partially covered by the advance of nature, also acts as a metaphor for the ultimate futility of so many grand Nazi schemes.

NUREMBERG KONGRESSHALLE, NUREMBERG, BAVARIA

Back in Nuremberg the largest remaining unfinished building from the Nazi era is the Kongresshalle (Congress Hall) which was, like the Deutsches Stadion, the product of monumental thinking. It was conceived as the indoor hall for party rallies capable of holding 50,000 people. This was a capacity far in excess of any other indoor space in the world at the time. Even today there is only one indoor arena of similar proportions – the Philippines Arena, opened in 2014, which has a capacity of 55,000.

The Nazis wanted a classically-proportioned indoor space for use during the annual party rallies to complement the outdoor Zeppelin Field. Modelled on the Coliseum in Rome, it was designed by the Nuremberg architects, Ludwig and Franz Ruff. The foundation stone was laid in 1935 and the building, had it been completed, would have reached a height of 70m and a diameter of 250m.

Construction was halted on the outbreak of war with the roofless building only half complete. Yet another grand design of the Third Reich came to nothing but more work had been done on the Congress Hall than any other of these visionary projects. The post-war fate of this building provoked the question of what to do with something that wasn't small

Representation of planned interior of Nuremberg Congress Hall which was designed to accommodate 50,000 people (Nürnberg Stadtarchiv)

Construction of the Nuremberg Congress Hall on the Rally Grounds site during 1939 (Nürnberg Stadtarchiv)

The Nuremberg Congress Hall today – it is the largest remaining Nazi-era building in Germany (Stefan Wagner)

enough to ignore and for which, unlike many Nazi structures, there was no obvious alternative.

Since 1945 this vast brooding structure, which has historic monument status, has produced a range of emotions and proposals for its future use. First there was a scheme to demolish it and later plans were made to convert it into a retail centre. Both ideas have been rejected.

Parts of the building are now in use. It has been a store for the Nuremberg Symphony Orchestra for many years and, since 2008, the orchestra has also staged a series of summer concerts in part of the outdoor space within the Congress Hall walls in an area known as the Serenadenhof. Most importantly, one end of the building houses the NS-Documentation Centre for the Rally Grounds (see Chapter One).

Once again a mixture of pragmatism and symbolism has determined the post-Third Reich use of the Congress Hall. It was a vast potentially suitable area and was therefore converted for use as storage space. Its historical significance is now acknowledged with the housing of the Documentation Centre within it. The staging of concerts there in the last few years also symbolises something else – that Nazi buildings, certainly those not tainted by terror, have been put to new uses without any apparent sense of impropriety.

SUMMARY

Many of the places featured in this section appear to symbolise the vanity and hyperbole of the Nazi leadership. Plans to build a stadium for 400,000 people and a Congress Hall for 50,000 seem vainglorious, unnecessary and inappropriate. Schemes to rebuild cities on a scale out of all proportion to their existing architecture offend many of our basic ideas of civic design and urban planning. The fact that most of these schemes never saw the light of day will be seen by most as a blessing.

It is also very difficult to separate the plans themselves from the motivations behind them. Surely only a dictatorial megalomaniac like Hitler could have dreamt up such ludicrously oversized projects. Countries and regimes do seek, whether consciously or otherwise, to immortalise themselves and their ideals through their architecture. Grand, overblown projects are not the exclusive preserve of dictatorships.

It is fascinating that some tantalising glimpses of these plans have survived. The load bearing test tower in Berlin, the concrete supports of the prototype Deutsches Stadion at Achtel and the still vast, albeit incomplete, Congress Hall in Nuremberg provide distressing reminders of what might have been.

CHAPTER SIX

War and Implosion
(Krieg und Götterdämmerung)

PREAMBLE

Almost every country in the world is littered with the relics of past wars and conflicts. The ruins of military installations created and left by the Second World War are a feature of many European countries. In this respect, Germany is little different to the nations against which it fought or whose territory it temporarily occupied. All created factories for war production, military command posts and defensive fortifications as part of their war effort. Some military relics from the Third Reich, however, are invested with more sinister overtones because of their association with Nazi ideology and, in particular, the use of forced labour at such sites.

The journey in this section mirrors the course of the war from the German perspective. Firstly, there were the dramatic early successes and conquests made possible by a vast rearmament programme which included civilian facilities, such as the newly opened VW factory, which were turned over to intense military production. A network of pens for housing U-boats was quickly established both in German ports like Bremen and also on the Atlantic coast as part of the 'Atlantic Wall'.

Later, as the tide of the war turned against Germany, increasingly desperate attempts were made to produce and deliver more armaments – with motorway tunnels at Engelberg turned into aircraft factories and secret factories like Reimahg built deep in the German countryside. Underground command and production complexes were built on a vast scale; 'Project Riese' in occupied Poland was one of these which was started but never completed.

We also have bequeathed to us the remains of the various command posts for Hitler and his generals established at places both inside and outside Germany including the so-called 'Wolf's Lair'. The site at which the July 1944 assassination plotters were executed also remains.

It is the use of forced labour which has been the defining issue in terms of the post-war legacy of these sites and decisions about how to deal with them. Combined with the role of German industry – including many of the most famous businesses in Germany today – this provokes continuing controversy.

VW FACTORY, WOLFSBURG, LOWER SAXONY.

In 2009, VfL Wolfsburg won the German Bundesliga for the first and so far only time. This footballing triumph somehow symbolised the coming of age of a city created just seventy years earlier during the Third Reich. Today Wolfsburg is one of the richest places in Germany and its gleaming skyline symbolises German prosperity. The city's journey from its foundation in 1938 to the present day epitomises many of the issues associated with the legacy of Nazism and Nazi architecture.   This was a whole new city created by the Nazis as an industrial centre for car manufacturing which became a major military production centre in the war effort.

The VW Beetle is often associated with Hitler but, although he ordered its original design and prototyping in the late 1930s, only after the end of the war did mass production begin as part of the Allies' attempts to restart the shattered German economy. Before the war, however, the factory and accompanying town were created from where the VW Beetle was to be

VW factory, Wolfsburg – VW is now one of the largest car manufacturers in the world (Andreas Praefcke)

Hitler opening the VW factory at Stadt des KdF-Wagens, (City of the Strength through Joy Car) 1938 (Bundesarchiv, unknown)

produced. Today we know it as Wolfsburg but it started life under the Nazis as Stadt des KdF-Wagens *(*Town of the Strength through Joy Car).

In 1934, Hitler awarded a contract to the car maker Ferdinand Porsche to create a 'Volkswagen' or 'People's Car'. Porsche, a naturalised German who had been born to German-speaking parents in what was then Czechoslovakia, had been involved in car production since its early days. Before 1933 he had set up his own car design business in Stuttgart. Hitler envisaged a small family car big enough for two adults and three children capable of travelling at 100km per hour on the planned German *Autobahn* network. It would be economical and available to buy through a savings scheme.

Various designs and prototypes were developed by Porsche and the decision was taken to open a new factory to start mass production. A site near the village of Fallersleben in Lower Saxony was identified because it was central, near a motorway and on a major railway line. This, however, was to be much more than just a factory. The Nazis wanted a whole new city and the architect Peter Koller was commissioned to design a garden city incorporating residential accommodation and ceremonial public spaces as well as the factory.

Hitler unveiled the foundation stone on 26 May 1938 with full-scale manufacturing of the 'People's Car' due to start in September 1939 – the very month the war began. As a result, the factory was soon turned over to military rather than civilian vehicle production. Hardly any VW Beetles were produced there in the year before the outbreak of war and only around 600 during the war which mainly went to the Nazi elite. Instead, the factory concentrated on vehicles useful to the war effort. There were two principal products – the Kübelwagen and the Schwimmwagen. Both these military vehicles used a chassis developed for the civilian car model and over 60,000 were produced.

During the war the factory also produced a range of other military hardware including tank chains, mines and, towards the end of the war, the V1 rocket. It was also a base for aircraft repair. Most of the workforce for the factory was forced labour including prisoners of war, pressed labourers from Nazi-occupied territories and, later, concentration camp inmates. It is estimated that as many as 20,000 forced labourers worked at VW during the war. Most lived in appalling conditions with many subjected to maltreatment often resulting in death.

For most of the conflict the factory escaped any serious bombing but, towards the end, it was severely damaged in Allied raids. The Americans captured the plant in 1945 and it was handed over to the British as part of their zone of occupation.

The decisions of the British occupiers in the very first weeks and months after the end of the war determined the future direction of the factory and the adjacent town. The original vision for the garden city had only been partially realised and the factory and some of the residential building had been completed without any of the planned ceremonial and public buildings. The British performed the first act of denazification by renaming the town Wolfsburg after the nearby castle.

Image used to promote the VW Beetle car which was only produced in significant numbers after the fall of the Nazis (Bundesarchiv, unknown)

Major Ivan Hirst, the British soldier who had been placed in charge of the VW factory, made a more important decision. The original plan of the Allies for post-war German industry had been to dismantle much of it and leave the country as a semi-pastoral nation to eliminate its capacity to be a major military power. Hirst, however, was fascinated by the VW Beetle and discovered that much of the machinery from the factory had survived the war because it had been moved to nearby buildings and avoided bomb damage. He persuaded his superiors that it would make sense to reopen the factory to make military vehicles for the British Army. Within a year the factory was producing 1,000 such vehicles a month.

Later, as tensions between the Western Allies and the Soviet Union developed, the British, Americans and French changed their policy towards German industry and decided to rebuild rather than restrict it. The object was to nurture a strong economy in the western sectors and REME, the Royal Electrical and Mechanical Engineers, of the British Army effectively ran the VW factory as it developed its civilian as well as military products. Hirst's contribution to the redevelopment of the VW factory has been commemorated with the naming of a street, Major-Hirst-Allee, not far from the plant.

It was, ironically, the British who finally realised Hitler's dream of a

'People's Car' and, after the factory was handed
back to German control in 1949, production of
the Beetle accelerated with the one-millionth car
coming off the assembly line in 1955. VW has
since developed into one of the most successful
vehicle manufacturers in the world with factories
in many countries. Wolfsburg has expanded
dramatically and now has a population of over
120,000. The theme park, opened in 2000, based
on the VW story called Autostadt now attracts
around two million visitors a year.

As the Nazi holiday area of Prora Rügen is
now becoming a tourist complex so has the VW
factory also reverted to its original purpose of
manufacturing civilian cars. This, though,
happened much more quickly in Wolfsburg and
it was partly the speed with which the factory and
the town were able to shake off their wartime role
that enabled the Nazi past, including the use of
forced labour, to be forgotten or at least ignored.

*Ferdinand Porsche, originator of
the VW Beetle, and later judged to
be 'Car Engineer of the Twentieth
Century' (Bundesarchiv, unknown)*

For Wolfsburg, 1945 really did seem like 'Stunde Null' or 'Year Zero'.

Peter Koller, the original architect who had designed Stadt des KdF-
Wagens, resumed where he had left off before 1939 and helped the redesign
and development. A new City Hall was opened in 1958 with no mention
on the plaque of the city's Nazi origins and in 1975 a book was published
about Wolfsburg which ignored the role of forced labour in the factory's
wartime operation.

From the mid-1980s onwards, as elsewhere in Germany, attitudes
towards the Nazi provenance of the factory and the city changed. In 1985 a
mass grave in which forced workers and concentration camp inmates had
been buried was rededicated. In 1990 a permanent exhibition about the Nazi
origins of Wolfsburg opened in the town's museum and 1999 saw the
opening of an exhibition in a former air-raid shelter beneath the factory
detailing VW's Nazi past. The company has publicly acknowledged its role
in the use of forced labour and paid compensation to victims. It has also
endowed various educational and welfare charities in the countries of origin
of forced labourers and in Israel.

The collaboration of many German industrialists with the Nazi regime
has been detailed over the past twenty to thirty years. This, as with so many
other such issues, had remained a taboo subject for many years. More
recently the complicity of German business has become a subject of fierce
and bitter debate. Household names of German industry, still in business

today, have often been accused of the use of forced labour in their factories during the Nazi period and many have admitted the charge and paid compensation to victims.

Ferdinand Porsche, once a member of the Nazi Party and of the SS, went to France after the war having been asked to set up production of the Beetle there but the scheme came to nothing. He was imprisoned for some time in France but allowed to return to his business in Stuttgart before he suffered a stroke and died in 1951. In 1996 he was posthumously admitted to the International Motorsports Hall of Fame and in 1999 he was named as Car Engineer of the Twentieth Century.

The story of Ferdinand Porsche, the founding of the Volkswagen factory and the creation of the VW Beetle car epitomise many of the issues associated with the legacy of Nazism and Nazi architecture. The return of the factory to its intended pre-war role is yet another example of the pragmatism which characterised the use of many Nazi buildings after the fall of the Third Reich. The attempt to wipe the Nazi story from the city and the company's history for many years after 1945 is also typical of much of the Nazi legacy. Since reunification, however, both Wolfsburg and VW have acknowledged that past and, in particular, the factory's use of forced labour as part of its history.

VALENTIN BUNKER, BREMEN.
An enormous rectangular structure on the Weser River on the approaches to the German port of Bremen is one of the most glaring remains of the German war machine of the Second World War. The Valentin submarine shelter, about 10km downstream from the centre of Bremen, broods over the area as a gaunt and ugly reminder of the Nazi legacy. It is just one of many U-boat pens in Germany and beyond which has survived and been put to a new use.

Valentin was one of the products of a massive German building programme undertaken from midway through the war to build vast protective shelters for the construction and repair of its vital U-boat fleet. Allied air superiority made it increasingly difficult to build or repair submarines in docks that were largely unprotected from air attacks. Work on Valentin started in 1943 using forced labour; its dimensions were impressive – 426m long, 97m wide, 27m high and with a roof that was 7m thick in parts. It was ninety per cent complete when the war ended and was the largest submarine shelter in Germany.

The human cost of the construction of Valentin was enormous. A combination of German criminals, forced labour from occupied territories and some concentration camp inmates was used. Workers were made to work gruelling twelve-hour shifts; some were housed in a nearby

The Valentin Bunker dominates the skyline across the Weser River on the approaches to Bremen (Oliku)

Forced labour was used extensively in the German war machine including at the Valentin submarine base in Bremen (Bundesarchiv, unknown)

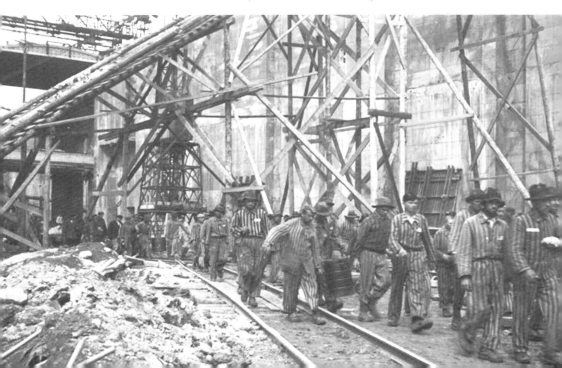

concentration camp in desperate living conditions. Between 10,000 and 12,000 people worked there during its construction period. The official death toll among workers was 553 but it is thought that the real number was probably more than ten times higher.

A second U-boat pen was also under construction in Bremen, the Hornisse bunker, and there were a series of others at German ports – in Hamburg, Kiel and Heligoland. A planned pen in Wilhelmshaven was never started. The construction programme was not confined to Germany. Pens were built in five ports in occupied France – Bordeaux, St. Nazaire, Brest, La Rochelle/La Pallice and Lorient and in Norway at Bergen and Trondheim. These fortifications in the occupied countries were part of the so-called 'Atlantic Wall' defence built along the entire north-western facing European coastline as a defence against the expected Allied invasion from Britain which, of course, eventually came on D-Day in 1944.

The Allies appreciated the strategic importance of these pens and most were the target of repeated bombing. A famous British raid in March 1942 severely damaged the fortified dock and U-boat pen at the French port of St. Nazaire. The Valentin in Bremen was hit twice in the closing stages of the war, first by British bombers on 27 March 1945 and three days later by the Americans. The severe damage done to the structure, including the breaching of the roof, caused the bunker to be abandoned by the Germans. No submarines were ever built at Valentin.

Today, the remains of many of these structures can still be seen. Their survival is a consequence both of the strength of their construction – and therefore difficulty of destruction – and pragmatic decisions taken first by the occupying Allies and later the Germans.

In 1945, the Valentin bunker became the responsibility of the British occupying forces. The original Allied plan was to demolish or to bury this

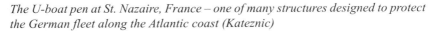

The U-boat pen at St. Nazaire, France – one of many structures designed to protect the German fleet along the Atlantic coast (Kateznic)

The Valentin bunker was extensively damaged by Allied bombing in March 1945 (Bundesarchiv, unknown)

and other structures. They were an unwanted reminder of the Nazis and their war machine. In some cases, this happened, most spectacularly at Heligoland on 18 April 1947 when the fortifications there were blown up in what is considered to have been the largest non-nuclear explosion in human history. Similarly, in Hamburg, one of the bunkers was destroyed. In Norway, the Bergen U-boat pen survived and is now used by the Norwegian Navy, and one of the bunkers in Trondheim remains. There are museums and commemorations at a number of the French U-boat pen sites.

In Bremen, however, attempts to demolish the bunkers ultimately failed. Bombing was tried but didn't work. Blasting was rejected as too dangerous to nearby communities. Both the British and the Americans used the bunkers as target practice in the period immediately after the end of the war and eventually Valentin was handed back to the German authorities.

Memorial to those who died and suffered at the Valentin Submarine bunker in Bremen (Jocian)

The debate in Bremen thereafter, about what to do with the Valentin, included plans to create an artificial hill by filling the remains with rubble or even using the building as a nuclear power station. Such proposals came to nothing and the more prosaic reality was that it was used first by the army as a training area and then became a supply depot for the German Navy from the 1960s until 2010.

As often for many years there was little attempt made in Bremen to acknowledge the dark past of this structure and, in particular, the sufferings of forced labourers. In 1983 a memorial plaque was erected there and opportunities were provided for former labourers who had survived the war to visit. Since its military use the historical significance of Valentin has been fully acknowledged. In a five year project it is being converted into Denkort Bunker Valentin with regular tours and educational programmes to explain its significance.

FLAKTOWERS BERLIN, HAMBURG AND VIENNA

The Germans applied similarly ambitious thinking to defending their cities from air attack as they did to protecting their submarine construction and repair. Many results of that thinking remain with us.

Construction of Flaktürme (Flaktowers) was ordered by Hitler after the RAF raids on Berlin in 1940. Three were built in Berlin and strategically sited to defend the city – the first at Berlin Zoo in the west, a second in the north at Humboldthain and a third at Friedrichshain in the east. Five more flaktowers were built, two in Hamburg and three in Vienna, and a number of smaller towers were constructed elsewhere; more were planned but never built.

Flaktowers were large towers on which powerful anti-aircraft guns could be mounted. They had walls 3.5m thick; some stood almost 40m high and their guns could deliver 8,000 rounds of fire a minute. They were also designed as air raid shelters capable of holding 10,000 people complete with a hospital ward. Each location had two towers – a 'G' Tower on which the guns were mounted and a smaller 'L' Tower which was a command tower and listening post with a retractable radar.

The strength of their construction and the scale of their armoury meant that most escaped any serious damage during the war; indeed, during the battle for Berlin in 1945, the three flaktowers were among the last places to surrender. One tower is said to have sheltered as many as 30,000 people.

After the war a number were completely or partly demolished by the Allies. In Berlin the Zoo towers were eventually blown up by the British after several failed attempts. That site is now part of Berlin Zoo and, in the partial remains of the Humboldthain tower, there is a climbing wall on the surviving face which is open to visitors. The Friedrichshain tower was

Anti-aircraft guns on a Berlin Flaktower during the height of the Second World War (Bundesarchiv, unknown)

A Hamburg Flaktower today – like most flaktowers, it has been retained and has new uses as a music school, shops and nightclub. (Unknown)

One of Hamburg's Flaktowers has been converted to a biomass energy plant (Unknown)

largely demolished and now lies under an artificial hillside in the Volkspark Friedrichshain.

One of the Hamburg Towers at Heiligengeistfeld contains a music school, shops and a nightclub. The other has been converted into a biomass heating plant. The two Vienna flaktowers remain – one is used by the Austrian Army and the other is an aquarium.

Among the architectural legacy of the Third Reich, the flaktowers are perhaps the least emotionally and politically charged relics. That some remain is largely because they were too difficult to demolish – a testament to how well they had been built. It is ironic that Albert Speer's vision of 'Ruin Value' buildings that would eventually produce aesthetically pleasing ruins has been realised with the surviving flaktowers.

REIMAHG FACTORY, WALPERSBERG, THURINGIA
From imposing submarine bunkers, giant wartime factories and impressive air defences all above ground our story now moves below ground to the first of many of the Third Reich's subterranean war facilities. These are often portrayed as being sinister by the very fact of being below the surface but they demonstrate Germany's continuing determination long after the tide had clearly turned against them.

'Reimahg' is an abbreviation for 'Reichsmarshall Hermann Göring, who commissioned the building of this underground aircraft factory in an old sand mine in the Walpersberg hills near the village of Kahla. Existing

Aircraft manufacture in 1945 inside the Reimahg Factory (named after Reichsmarshall Hermann Göring) (Bundesarchiv, unknown)

tunnels in the hillside were enlarged and other tunnels and large concrete bunkers were built. A runway 1,000m long was constructed on top of the hillside. The main factory covered an area of 250,000 square metres.

The factory was to build the Messerschmitt ME262 jet plane which was vital to the German war effort. Existing Messerschmitt factories were not producing them fast enough and were vulnerable to Allied air attack. The Reimahg factory operated under the codename 'Lachs' (salmon) and used forced labour. Around 12,000 people were involved in building the factory and 1,000 are thought to have died working there. The factory only produced twenty-seven ME262s.

After the war, the Reimahg plant fell within the Soviet occupation zone. The Russians demolished much of it and sealed the entrances. The remains of the underground plant were first used to store food and later became a storage area for geological researchers. The East Germans returned the site to military use in the mid-1970s to store ammunition and weapons close to the West German border and, for a while after reunification, this military use continued.

During the GDR era various commemorative events were held and memorials erected to the victims of Reimahg. As with many Nazi sites in East Germany these commemorations were part of the regime's political

Blocked up entrances to remains of the Reimahg factory at Walpersberg (Unknown)

narrative – the deliverance of Germany from fascism by Communism. Since reunification commemoration has continued, albeit with a different tone. In 2005 an association was formed by local people interested in uncovering more of Reimahg's history and parts of its remains are open to visitors.

ENGELBERG TUNNEL, LEONBERG, NEAR STUTTGART, BADEN-WÜRTTEMBERG.

Another underground war facility, this time a motorway tunnel, provides a further example of the increasingly desperate attempts to harness all available resources to reverse the worsening war situation.

The Engelberg twin-tunnels had been opened on 5 November 1938 as part of the rapid development of the German Autobahn network. This, Germany's first autobahn tunnel, was 318m long on the road between Stuttgart and Heilbronn. In 1944 both were closed to traffic and converted into a factory to make parts for the Messerschmitt ME262.

An extra floor was built inside the tunnel to provide a total of over 11,000 square metres of working space. This factory also relied on forced labour – much of it brought from a concentration camp in occupied France. It is estimated that 3,000 people worked there and there were 374 recorded deaths. Just before the end of the war the machinery was removed and the tunnels blown up by the Germans as the Allies advanced.

Memorial to the victims of forced labour in the Engelberg Tunnel (K.Jahne)

Blocked up tunnel entrance to the remains of the Engelberg Tunnel now no longer part of the motorway network (K.Jahne)

After the war both tunnels were restored – one very quickly and the other by the early 1960s. By the 1990s, however, they had become a bottleneck on the motorway and in 1999 new larger twin-tunnels were opened and the autobahn diverted. One original tunnel was filled in with rubble from the building of the new tunnels but the other remained accessible. The plan to use it as a new bypass for the town of Leonberg came to nothing.

A memorial was, meanwhile, established at the south exit in memory of the forced labourers who died in the tunnel and is maintained by the group that looks after the memorial at the site of the nearby Leonberg Concentration Camp.

PROJECT RIESE COMPLEX, POLAND

The most extreme example of the Nazis' attempts to 'go underground' to preserve their slim chances of victory as the war turned against them are to be found buried beneath ground in what is now Poland. 'Project Riese' was an attempt to build one of the largest military-industrial complexes underground that the world has ever seen. That, like so many Nazi schemes, could not turn the tide of the war and remained uncompleted. It was conceived on a truly vast scale and, yet again, relied on forced labour. Many thousands suffered and as many as 5,000 people are thought to have died in the pursuit of another ultimately futile effort to avoid defeat.

Project Riese was an ambitious attempt by the Nazis to create an underground military complex on a scale hitherto unseen (Info Poland, unknown)

The project started in 1943 and appears to have had two objectives – the creation of underground industrial complexes for the war effort and also a subterranean military command headquarters. Seven different parts of the complex were started – all in the Owl Mountains in Lower Silesia.

Project Riese centred on what is now Ksiaz Castle at Walbrzych in Lower Silesia but which, at the time, was known as Schloss Fürstenstein. The castle itself was adapted and a vast network of tunnels, underground halls and a narrow gauge railway were blasted beneath the surface to create the complex. Much of the work was done by Polish and Russian forced labourers, prisoners of war and, later, by concentration camp inmates. The castle had been confiscated by the Nazis earlier in the war and the considerable modifications were designed to make it the centre of this buried complex. It is also believed to have been intended as an elaborate new eastern headquarters for the Führer.

Remains of the interior of Project Riese – tour companies now offer visits inside this vast underground complex (Info Poland, unknown)

The underground areas of the complex in the surrounding countryside were at Rzeczka, Wlodarz, Osowka, Sokolec, Jugowice, Gluszyca and Sobon. Most of these appear to have been linked to each other by narrow gauge railways and tunnels. Up to 100 sub-camps of the KZ-Gross-Rosen concentration camp were built to house the forced labourers.

After the war the tunnels and underground spaces were taken over by the Soviet and Polish armies and stripped of their useful materials. Ksiaz Castle can now be accessed to view some of the workings and underground tours are also organized to parts of the Project Riese complex.

Many rumours and myths still persist about Project Riese. Was it a secret underground test site for nuclear weapons? Was it actually much bigger than we believe? Are there many more underground areas not yet discovered? Was it a centre for looted art treasures? As time elapses it is doubtful whether these questions will ever be answered.

WOLF'S LAIR, KETRZYN, POLAND

Wherever the Führer went his headquarters accompanied him. During the war he spent comparatively little time in his capital city and more than 800 days at the Wolfsschanze (Wolf's Lair) so-called because 'Wolf' was Hitler's nickname. The Wolf's Lair, near what was then Rastenburg (now Ketrzyn in Poland), was Hitler's main Eastern Headquarters but only one of as many as ten fortified headquarters he and his entourage occupied during the War.

As well as the Wolfsschanze, the most well-known and most used of these Führerhauptquartiere (Führer Headquarters), were the Führerbunker in Berlin (see Chapter Eight) and the Berghof near Berchtesgaden (see Chapter Two). There were others – Alderhorst was used during the Ardennes offensive, and Felsennest, near Bad Münstereifel, in 1939 and 1940 during the Battle of France. There were bunkers at Tannenberg in the Black Forest, Vinnytsia in the Ukraine, Bruly-de-Pesche in Belgium and Margival in France. A specially fortified train or Führersonderzug served as headquarters during the Balkans campaign and was later Hitler's main transport between Berlin, Munich and other bases.

It is, however, the *Wolfsschanze* which has a special place in Nazi history as the base from which Hitler directed much of the latter part of the war. First used in June 1941 it covered two and half square kilometres and was the base for over 2,000 people. A heavy camouflage of trees and vegetation gave the appearance of continuous woodland from the air.

There were three security zones. The innermost comprised Hitler's bunker and those of the other top Nazi leaders. Each of the bunkers was made from steel-reinforced concrete. A second security zone housed the bunkers of the next tier of Nazi leaders and there was a third outer zone of

Hitler at the Wolf's Lair where the Führer spent the best part of three years during the War (Bundesarchiv, Reprich)

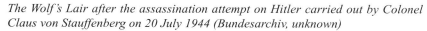

The Wolf's Lair after the assassination attempt on Hitler carried out by Colonel Claus von Stauffenberg on 20 July 1944 (Bundesarchiv, unknown)

fortifications. The area was served by a nearby airfield and railway lines. There was extensive personal security for Hitler and the whole complex was guarded by special protection units as well as landmines. Hitler controlled the Russian campaign from the Wolf's Lair where he spent more time than anywhere else after June 1941. We do not know if the Allies knew of its location but it was never hit by their bombing.

The Wolfsschanze was, however, attacked from within. It was the scene of the most famous attempt on Hitler's life and probably the one that came closest to success. Colonel Claus von Stauffenberg carried a suitcase containing a bomb into the daily military conference on 20 July 1944 and left it under a table close to Hitler. The bomb exploded, caused serious damage and four deaths but the Führer survived with only minor injuries.

Hitler and the Nazi leadership stayed at the Wolf's Lair for a few more months but, with the Soviet armies advancing from the east, the complex was evacuated in November 1944. The Wehrmacht were ordered to demolish it and did so in January 1945. The size and strength of the buildings resulted in only partial success of the destruction and the Wolfsschanze fell into Soviet hands. After the war the Russians destroyed most of the complex – a process which took almost a decade.

After the fall of Communism unofficial tours were made of the remains by a private company which controlled the area but in 2012 an official museum with stronger educational content was opened on the site and a plaque now commemorates the '20 July Plot'.

Remains of the Wolf's Lair near Ketrzyn in Poland which can now be toured by visitors (Albert Jankowski)

BENDLERBLOCK, BERLIN

The attempt to kill Hitler in his forest redoubt, previously considered to be impregnable, was masterminded almost 700km away at a building in the Tiergarten district of Berlin.

The building was the Bendlerblock which had originally been built as the headquarters of the Imperial German Navy in 1914. It was named after Johann Christoph Bendler – a Prussian landowner and Berlin City Councillor. After the First World War it became the headquarters of the German Army, a role which was expanded after the Nazis came to power in 1933, and served as the base for several departments of the Wehrmacht High Command during the war.

It was here that 'Operation Valkyrie' was masterminded. Originally this was a contingency plan developed by the Wehrmacht to maintain order in the event of a breakdown of civil order in wartime Germany. It was, however, modified by a group of high-ranking officers with access to the plan. They plotted to assassinate Hitler and install a new leadership in Germany to make peace with the Allies. The leaders were General Friedrich Olbricht, Major General Henning von Tresckow and Claus von Stauffenberg. On the very evening of 20 July 1944 the conspirators were summarily executed in the courtyard of the Bendlerblock.

The Bendlerblock building in 1944 – headquarters of various Wehrmacht departments (Bundesarchiv – unknown)

Memorial to German Resistance at the Bendlerblock on the spot where the 20 July plotters were executed (unknown)

Bendlerblock building today – as well as being a memorial site, it is home to the German Federal Defence Ministry (Beek 100)

In the final days of the war, the Bendlerblock was used as a military command post; it surrendered to the Russians but, under the occupation agreement, became part of the western sector of Berlin. Part of it now houses the Memorial to the German Resistance – a museum chronicling not only the '20 July Plot' but all resistance during the Third Reich. A plaque in the courtyard commemorates the site of the plotters' execution. Since German reunification many other parts of the building have become the home of the Federal Defence Ministry.

Makers of the 2008 Tom Cruise film *Valkyrie,* which told the story of the '20 July Plot', were given permission to film the execution scenes in the Bendlerblock courtyard.

SUMMARY

A number of themes emerge from the venues associated with the war effort featured in this section.

The strong theme of pragmatism again reasserts itself regarding the reuse and reinvention of Nazi-era buildings and sites. Some of these sites were useful in the immediate aftermath of a devastating war either to the occupying Allies or to the Germans as they retook control of their country – a vehicle factory in Wolfsburg, a submarine bunker site in Bremen and a motorway tunnel near Stuttgart.

A second theme is also a very practical one. Although the demolition of the military installations of the Third Reich was agreed among the Allies this agreement was occasionally ignored or proved too difficult to execute. Some Nazi military structures were so armoured and built on such a scale that they resisted all attempts at demolition. The partial remains of the flaktowers in Berlin, Hamburg and Vienna have new, generally unrelated, uses as aquariums, night clubs and climbing walls.

A number of venues not intended for reuse, and for which there was a positive desire for demolition, also proved resilient. Hence the Wolf's Lair in Poland (and some other Führer headquarters) and the remains of both Reimahg and Project Riese are still with us after seventy years.

The third and most important theme is the attitude taken by post-war Germany to the use of forced labour at almost all the venues. In the past twenty or so years there has been recognition of the thousands who suffered and died in appalling conditions in these places of forced service to the Reich's war effort. This, as with other aspects of the Nazi legacy, was substantially ignored by Germany for many post-war years. More recently, however, memorials and museums have been established at many of the factories once using forced labour. A number of companies have also paid compensation to victims, survivors and related charities.

Finally, the memorialisation of the Bendlerblock in Berlin, where the unsuccessful plotters were executed, demonstrates another theme. For many years the celebration of resistance to the Nazis was not a major factor – certainly not in West Germany before reunification where commemorating the few who resisted the Nazis only served to highlight the guilt of the many who had collaborated or turned a blind eye. With the passage of time this has changed and resistance to the Nazis is now part of the narrative surrounding the legacy of the Third Reich.

CHAPTER SEVEN

Holocaust

(Holocaust)

PREAMBLE

The scale of the planned extermination of European Jewry by Nazi Germany in pursuit of its unbridled racist ideology was so vast and remains so unbearably incomprehensible that it almost defies description. The Holocaust was brutally simple in its objective but complicated, far-reaching and devastating in its impact. The terrible implementation happened over several years at a range of locations both inside and outside Germany. On this journey, I am confining myself to four defining locations which, each in their own way, say something important about this unrelenting and systematic terror.

Genocide was, sadly, far from the unique preserve of the Third Reich and there have been many subsequent examples. There is something particularly chilling, however, about the acts of cruelty perpetrated by Nazi Germany which took place within the lifetime of my parents and a few years before my own birth.

Particularly chilling is, of course, the magnitude of the numbers of victims but it is also the frighteningly bureaucratic efficiency with which the Holocaust was carried out that renders it unique. This last point puts the Wannsee Memorial House on the outskirts of Berlin on a vital and fascinating pedestal of evil in this story; it is literally where the 'Final Solution' began.

In an earlier chapter the first Nazi concentration camp at Dachau was featured. It was an awful place of torture and terror where many died but it was not an extermination camp. In this section the focus is on those places which were deliberately set up as killing factories. There were so many that any selection is almost arbitrary but I have chosen the place of the best-known of the Nazi death camps, Auschwitz in Poland. Sachsenhausen, not far from Berlin, is also important in the post-war story of these places.

Finally, there were of course tales of great heroism and sacrifice associated with those who tried to save people from the gas chambers. The factory at Brnenec, currently in the Czech Republic, merits special note because it belonged to Oskar Schindler.

Railway lines leading to the Auschwitz extermination camp – the image which has come to symbolise the Holocaust (Angelo Celedon)

WANNSEE MEMORIAL HOUSE, BERLIN

Wannsee House can, viewed at a distance across a peaceful lake, be mistaken for an ordinary Prussian country house. It looks the model of respectability, of normality and of civilisation in the genteel south-western suburbs of the German capital. Just for one day in its history, however, it was the venue for a meeting which had as far-reaching and calamitous consequences as any in history.

The villa at 56-58 Am Grossen, Wannsee was a mansion built as the residence of a local factory owner in 1914. The SS bought it in 1940 as a guest house and used it for meetings and conferences. This was the address to which the Director of the Reich Main Security Office, Obergruppenführer Reinhard Heydrich, summoned fourteen men on Tuesday 20 January 1942 to determine the fate of millions of Jews across German-occupied Europe.

The conference was originally scheduled for December 1941 but had been postponed because of the Japanese attack on Pearl Harbour and the United States' subsequent entry into the war. Its purpose was straightforward – to agree arrangements to implement the extermination of the Jews.

It is believed that the principle of extermination had, by implication, been agreed beforehand and the purpose of the meeting was to knock heads together between the various government agencies to ensure there were no objectors. The minutes of the meeting, the formal part of which lasted only

Wannsee House, Berlin, outwardly a respectable suburban house which was the scene of one of the most deadly meetings in human history (A.Savin)

an hour and a half, are couched in coded official language but their meaning is clear. After the meeting the participants drank cognac to toast their work!

This event was part of a pattern of Jewish persecution going back to the early days of the regime. The Nuremberg Laws introduced in 1935 had deprived German Jews of many of their rights. Kristallnacht in November 1938 was the 'highpoint' of an orgy of violence against Jewish people and property inside Germany. When those fifteen men assembled at Wannsee in January 1942 the extra-judicial killing of Jews, as well as others considered 'subhuman' and the Nazis' political opponents, was already widespread. Wannsee formalised and made it official policy to ensure that the plan was ruthlessly implemented with different parts of the Nazi machine cooperating with one another.

Historians argue about who authorised the 'Final Solution' as there is no direct evidence linking it to Hitler. Heydrich, however, must have

Reinhard Heydrich, organiser of the Wannsee Conference, which confirmed the 'Final Solution' for the extermination of the Jews of Europe (Bundesarchiv, unknown)

been responding, either to direct orders or at least clear encouragement, when he issued the invitations to the conference.

Entering the conference room in the Wannsee Memorial House today is curiously almost as chilling as visiting concentration camps. The matter of fact way the conference participants discussed a plan to kill millions of people in an incongruously pleasant setting makes it all the more poignant. Their approach that it was another mere bureaucratic and organisational challenge makes comprehension all the more difficult.

The Wannsee House has been a memorial site since 1992. The visitor can walk inside the room where the meeting took place and elsewhere in the house there is information about the conference and the wider Nazi story. Plans for its future redevelopment are to sharpen the focus on the specific events there as other Holocaust memorials and public sites tell the more general Nazi story.

The struggle to get this historic address recognised as a landmark was lengthy. The initial post-war use was by the Allied occupation forces after which it became an educational centre. From the mid-1960s the historian Joseph Wulf tried to get the house registered as a Holocaust memorial centre but, frustrated by lack of progress, he committed suicide in 1974. Only in

Inside the room at the Wannsee House where the 'Final Solution' was decided and which is now a museum and memorial (Seth Schoen)

1992, on the fiftieth anniversary of the conference, did the dedications as a memorial site and educational centre occur. In 2006 a permanent exhibition was opened.

Wannsee is the ultimate 'perpetrator site' from the Nazi period. There were no victims tortured or killed here. In the ongoing debate in Germany about the distinction between 'perpetrator' and 'victim' sites the latter tend to be more directly supported financially by the Federal and *Land* governments and generally do not charge admission to visitors. Wannsee is an exception in that it does receive ongoing financial support from both the Federal and Berlin governments. Admission charges are made at many, but not all, perpetrator sites although, to tell the story of the terror wrought by the Nazis for this and future generations, both 'victim' and 'perpetrator' sites have a role to play and both need support.

AUSCHWITZ EXTERMINATION CAMP, near OSWIECIM, POLAND

Auschwitz has become the defining international symbol of the Holocaust and an international place of pilgrimage and remembrance of the extra-judicial murder by Nazi Germany of six million Jewish people and many millions of others. In the context of the post-1945 story the significance of Auschwitz is not only that it was the largest and most deadly camp complex but also because of its geography and history since 1945.

Ceremony at Auschwitz, January 2015 to mark the 70th anniversary of the liberation of the extermination camp (BBC, unknown)

Holocaust researchers have produced wildly differing estimates of the number of Nazi camps with figures ranging from 7,000 to 42,000. This is partly a problem of definition because there were many different types of camps from prisoner of war camps through to extermination camps. The consensus among most respected researchers, however, is that there were at least 15,000 camps and sub-camps of various sorts established by the Nazis in Germany and the countries they occupied during their twelve year period of power.

Most of these camps were destroyed – often by the Nazis themselves but also by the Allies after the war. There is a continuing debate about why the Allies did not attempt to destroy them during the war. Reasonably strong evidence exists that the Allies were aware, certainly by 1944, of the scale of mass killing in the Nazi death camps but there is less agreement among historians about why nothing was done about it. Some argue that it was a pragmatic decision based on the perceived chances of success of a precision bombing raid. Others take the view that the Allies believed it would be a risky diversion of resources from the main war effort. Some suggest that the decision not to bomb Auschwitz and other camps reveals a lack of interest or concern or even a latent anti-Semitism.

The basic facts about Auschwitz are well-known. It was a complex of three main camps – Auschwitz 1, Auschwitz 2-Birkenau (the main extermination camp) and Auschwitz 3-Monowitz (a forced labour camp established by the company IG Farben) as well as forty-five sub-camps. Many of the sub-camps were established to provide forced labour for other German companies who established factories in the area to support the production of armaments for the war effort.

The Auschwitz camp was first established on the site of a former Polish army barracks in 1940 and was liberated by Soviet troops on 27 January 1945 – a day which has subsequently became International Holocaust Remembrance Day. In the five years of its existence, more than one million people are thought to have died there – over ninety per cent of them Jewish. Jews were transported there from Germany and German-occupied Europe and most perished in the gas chambers there. Others died through malnutrition, disease, forced labour or as victims of medical experiments.

After its liberation in January 1945 the Auschwitz complex was first used as a hospital for camp survivors. The Russians and Poles gathered evidence of war crimes and eventually about fifteen per cent of the camp guards and staff were brought to trial including the camp commander, Rudolf Höss, who was convicted and hanged at the site in 1947. The IG Farben factory was dismantled by the Russians and taken to the Soviet Union.

The site of the former death camp was declared a museum and memorial

Surviving prisoners at Auschwitz which was liberated by Soviet troops on 27 January 1945 (Russian Government Archive, unknown)

site by Poland as early as 1947 and in 1955 a permanent exhibition was opened. The speed of its establishment stands in marked contrast to the time taken to establish memorials or museums at former concentration camps inside Germany. This illustrates an important paradox in the story of what has happened to concentration camp sites after 1945. In West Germany only pressure from survivors and from the families of victims eventually led to commemoration at these sites some years later. In Poland, however, the Communist post-war government wished to highlight their preferred narrative of communist liberation from the evils of fascism. This was true of many Nazi concentration camp sites in Communist-controlled Eastern Europe where memorials were quickly established. Whatever the political motives, the outcome was that the marking of the historical significance of Auschwitz was underway within two years of the camp's liberation.

In 1979 UNESCO declared the area a World Heritage Site. Almost one and a half million people visit it annually. In January 2015 more than 3,000 people, including 300 survivors and the German President, Joachim Gauck, gathered at the Auschwitz site to mark the seventieth anniversary of its liberation.

SACHSENHAUSEN CONCENTRATION CAMP, near
ORANIENBURG, BRANDENBURG

The Sachsenhausen Concentration Camp also fell within the Communist-controlled side of the Iron Curtain after 1945. Its post-war story illustrates another important point about the fate of some of the concentration camp sites after the end of the Third Reich – their reuse by the 'opposite side' as detention camps, even as places of terror.

Sachsenhausen was established as a concentration camp in 1936 at the town of Oranienburg about 35km from Berlin. It replaced an earlier camp in the town and its initial focus was to house political prisoners and as a training centre for the SS. Gas chambers were installed in the middle of the war and it is estimated that around 30,000 people died there either from starvation, medical experimentation, forced labour or execution. Industrial plants were established nearby, as so frequently, for which the camp supplied labour. One such business, a brick works, is believed to have supplied materials in preparation for the rebuilding of Berlin as Welthauptstadt Germania (see Chapter Five).

The story of terror and death at Sachsenhausen under the Nazis is not unlike that of most Nazi extermination camps but a particularly shocking feature of its history is that the terror did not end in 1945. The Soviet occupying forces took over the camp and it became NKVD Special Camp

Memorial to those who died and suffered at Sachsenhausen Concentration Camp near Oranienburg (Sachsenhausen Memorial Site, unknown)

Prisoners' clothes at Sachsenhausen – such images went round the world in the Spring of 1945 and made people aware of the scale of the Holocaust (Bundesarchiv, O.Ang)

Number Seven – one of a network of camps run by the Soviet Secret Service. Most of these were set up in former Nazi concentration camps. From 1945 until 1950, an estimated 60,000 people were held in Sachsenhausen including German Army officers captured by the Allies, Nazi functionaries and also people seen as enemies of the communists. During the five years of its existence, Special Camp Number Seven increasingly shifted its emphasis from being a place to hold suspected Nazis to one for incarcerating the enemies of the new regime.

Conditions were harsh with many people dying of disease and malnutrition; executions and deportations to the Soviet Union were also frequent. In 1990, after the collapse of the Berlin Wall had ended the

Museum established at Sachsenhausen about the Soviet-era camp – one of the Nazi camps which became Soviet concentration camps after the end of the Second World War (K.Scaetze)

Communist regime in East Germany, mass graves were discovered at Sachsenhausen containing 12,000 bodies – most thought to be victims of the five year period of Soviet use of the site.

Dispute among historians continues about the true numbers held by the Soviet Union in the ten similar camps across the Soviet Zone in East Germany. In 1990 the Russians released figures claiming that the total figure was just over 150,000 of whom 42,000 died of disease or starvation and 756 were executed. More recent German estimates suggest increased numbers both of detainees and deaths.

After the camp closed in 1950 some of the remaining inmates were handed over to the new East German government and put on trial. The camp itself became a police and army base for a number of years. In 1961 a memorial was opened on the site to commemorate the victims of the Nazi camp to which, after reunification, a full museum was added.

A separate museum at Sachsenhausen now covers its period as a Soviet detention camp. The Russians cooperated by allowing access to their archives but their Foreign Ministry declined an invitation to the opening. They claimed that it was wrong to equate the crimes of fascism with the actions of the Soviet occupation authorities during denazification.

The story of Sachsenhausen is part of a live debate in Germany now about the relative treatments of the Nazi and the Communist legacies of twentieth-century German history. There are arguments that too little regard is given to the sufferings of East Germans under the Communist dictatorship for almost fifty years after 1945. This is linked to a wider discussion in Eastern Europe about the need to recognise the sufferings of people elsewhere during the Cold War period.

There are memorials and museums dedicated to the communist period in Germany including the Hohenschönhausen Memorial in Berlin – previously the headquarters of the notorious East German secret police, the Stasi. These are relatively few compared with the memorialisation of Nazi sites and comparison and judgement of different levels of evil is a difficult task. The greater emphasis currently given to the Third Reich is partly a reflection of the passage of time. The communist regime in East Germany may be too fresh in people's minds and therefore not ready for the treatment now generally accorded the Nazi period.

SCHINDLER FACTORIES, BRNENEC, CZECH REPUBLIC AND KRAKOW, POLAND

The story of the Holocaust recounts unremitting torture, slavery, murder and genocide. Yet within this awful narrative there are examples of courage, resistance and bravery. One is that of Oskar Schindler whose exploits were celebrated in the 1993 Steven Spielberg film, *Schindler's List.* The factories

Oskar Schindler's original 'Emalia' Factory in Krakow in Poland where he protected many Jews from the Nazis (Noa Cafri)

where Schindler saved many Jews from the Holocaust are therefore important places in the architectural legacy of the Third Reich.

Oskar Schindler was born in Moravia in what is now the Czech Republic in 1908. After a series of jobs, a spell in the Czech Army and a chequered early life including an alcohol problem, Schindler became a member of the Sudeten German Party in 1935. The party favoured the assimilation of the German-speaking areas of Czechoslovakia into a pan-German state. He became a spy for German intelligence and was arrested by the Czech authorities but later released under the terms of the Munich Agreement.

Schindler became a member of the Nazi Party; he continued to spy for the Germans and worked mainly on the Czech-Polish border where he acquired useful intelligence which aided the German invasion of Poland in 1939. At the same time he acquired an enamelware factory in Krakow which came to be known by its shortened nickname of Emalia. He employed Jews as well as Poles in the factory. His original motives were probably financial as he could pay less to Jewish people.

Oskar Schindler, a Nazi Party member whose exploits to save Jews were immortalised in the film 'Schindler's List'. (unknown)

He decided, however, that, despite being a member of the Nazi party, the persecution of the Jews was unjustified and he used his position to protect them from deportation and death. Through a combination of bribery, persuasion and influence, and, despite the efforts of the local Nazi authorities, he managed to keep his Jewish workers partly because his business's contracts to supply enamelware to the military were deemed crucial to the war effort. When the Krakow Jewish Ghetto, where many of his workers lived, was due to be liquidated he protected his Jewish staff by allowing them to stay at the factory overnight. After the ghetto's destruction Schindler persuaded the local Nazi leaders to allow him to build a sub-camp for the nearby concentration camp within the Emalia factory. Schindler's Jews not only survived but were able to enjoy acceptable living conditions and decent nutrition.

Perhaps most astonishingly, in 1944, he obtained permission to relocate his entire factory away from the front line of the advancing Soviet forces to Brünnlitz (now Brnenec) in what is now the Czech Republic. There he could shield his Jewish workers from deportation to the death camps using access to the black market and bribery to keep Nazi officials sweet. Some 1,200 Jews on the so-called 'Schindler's List' were transported from Krakow to Brünnlitz and lived there in relative safety until the end of the war.

Despite his bravery in saving many Jews he remained a member of the Nazi Party and therefore risked arrest after the war but he made his way to Germany where he settled. The remainder of his life was not easy. He lived for some years in Germany surviving on money from Jewish organisations and later migrated to Argentina where his business ventures were unsuccessful. He returned to Germany where he died in 1974. He was awarded the title of 'Righteous among the Nations' by the state of Israel for his work in saving Jews from the Holocaust and is buried in Jerusalem.

The sites of the two Schindler factories have subsequently enjoyed contrasting fortunes. The Krakow site became a telecommunications factory

Schindler's factory at Brnenec in the Czech Republic – he relocated his factory there and continued to protect Jews from deportation to extermination camps (Miaow Miaow)

Dereliction at Schindler's factory at Brnenec – campaigns are underway to preserve the historic site (Times of Israel, unknown)

soon after the war. This survived until 2002 and, in 2010, a museum was opened on the site dedicated to the wartime Nazi occupation of Krakow and Schindler's role in saving Jews at his factory.

The factory in what is now Brnenec in the Czech Republic is currently a site of industrial dereliction. It was for many years a state-run textiles business called Vitka supplying seat covers for the car and aviation industries. After the fall of communism the business changed hands several times and eventually went bankrupt in 2004 since when the site has remained empty. The local Mayor has developed plans for a Holocaust Museum and memorial but his request for government funding remains unsuccessful. The buildings are still the subject of a legal dispute and serious concerns remain that this historically significant site may not be saved.

SUMMARY

The Holocaust, and its commemoration, remains the subject of international attention. Although the term specifically refers to the mass murder of six million Jews by Nazi Germany, the remembrance of the Holocaust is now often bound up with the broader concept of genocide including more recent examples of racially motivated mass murder and ethnic cleansing in places such as the former Yugoslavia, Rwanda and the Middle East.

In Germany, and the lands occupied by the Nazis, the way in which the specific physical legacy of the Holocaust has been handled reveals several key facts. Faced with defeat they destroyed many concentration and extermination camps as they sought to remove evidence of their mass murder and genocide. The Allies, shocked by what they discovered in 1945, demolished many more camps. Pragmatism, and something more sinister, frequently came into play. Once their remaining victims had been cared for the camps were considered useful sites to house suspected Nazis and, in other cases, refugees – accordingly many were pressed back into service. In the case of ten sites in the Soviet occupation zone, including Sachsenhausen, they were run for up to five years after the war as brutal places of detention where deaths and executions occurred under a new dictatorship.

The establishment of memorials on the sites of Nazi concentration and extermination camps was recognised as important soon after the war. In Poland and in other Communist-controlled countries, including East Germany, political interest assisted the process. Commemorating the victims of fascism fitted the narrative of regimes eager to portray the idea of Communism liberating countries from Nazi rule.

The response was different in what became West Germany. Here official attitudes were more ambivalent and part of a wider phenomenon of ignoring the Nazi past through a combination of guilt, complicity and the pressure of post-war survival. Often survivor and victim pressure were predominant in the eventual memorialisation of these sites.

It should be noted, as a postscript, that a slow and painful process occurred in coming to terms with the Holocaust in other Nazi occupied countries. There was widespread collaboration with the German occupiers in France, the Netherlands, the Channel Islands and elsewhere. Only more recently has France, for example, acknowledged the role played by collaborators in sending French Jews to the death camps. A memorial was established in 1977 at the notorious internment camp at Drancy in Paris from which over 60,000 Jews were deported to their death during the German occupation of France.

CHAPTER EIGHT

Downfall
(Untergang)

PREAMBLE

An enduringly fascinating question about the Second World War is why the
Germans fought so desperately – well beyond the moment when any
reasonable chance of victory had disappeared. Many hundreds of thousands
of extra lives were lost and German cities reduced to rubble in the last
months of a war that had by then only one possible outcome. It has
sometimes been claimed that the Allies' insistence on total unconditional
surrender was the reason that Germany fought to the bitter end. Ian
Kershaw, in his study of this question *'The End – Germany 1944-45'* argues

*Site of the Führerbunker in Berlin – now a carpark next to an apartment block
(Colin Philpott)*

that there were many factors which contributed to Germany's resistance. These included lingering popular backing for Hitler; the terror still being exercised by the regime, particularly at local level, to keep people in line; the dread of occupation by the Soviet Union; and a sense of duty among senior military and state officials which continued even after their belief in Nazism had evaporated.

However, Kershaw concludes that it was the nature of the Nazi state built around the cult of personality of the Führer that was the decisive factor. He wrote that 'Hitler's mass charismatic appeal had long since dissolved, but the structures and mentalities of his charismatic rule lasted until his death in the bunker. The dominant elites, divided as they were, possessed neither the collective will nor the mechanisms of power to prevent Hitler taking Germany to total destruction.'

With the benefit of hindsight we now can divine a sense of reckless hopelessness to last-ditch efforts of the Third Reich to recover. In this final chapter we look at two places associated with the period when the Nazi state imploded. Firstly Peenemünde, the V2 rocket site, from which launches were made principally targeting Britain in Hitler's last desperate throw of the dice. Secondly, the Reich Chancellery and its associated bunker in Berlin where Hitler tried to exercise command in a manner increasingly detached from reality.

We also take a look at the location of two iconic events which did much to shape the course of post-war Germany and the attitudes of Germans to the Nazi legacy – the British bombing of Dresden and the British liberation of Bergen-Belsen.

PEENEMÜNDE ROCKET SITE, USEDOM, MECKLENBURG-VORPOMMERN

Peenemünde has a central place in the Nazi story and is also an iconic location in the history of twentieth-century technology.

The V2 rocket or 'Vergeltungswaffe 2' *(*Vengeance Weapon 2) has come to symbolise the last-ditch attempts by Nazi Germany to stave off defeat. Between September 1944 and March 1945, more than 3,000 were fired over half of which were aimed at London. 2,754 civilians were killed in London by V2s and 6,523 people injured. They were also aimed at liberated areas of Belgium, the Netherlands and France; some V2s were even fired at Germany itself as the Allies advanced into the Reich.

The impact of the V2 on the military outcome of the war was minimal but, for people living in London and other parts of South-East England and East Anglia, the V2 induced great terror late in the war. Their cost in money and resources for Germany was considerable. One estimate says that each V2 cost the equivalent of £2.5 million at 2015 prices. For Hitler, though,

Launch of a V2 rocket at Peenemünde test site in 1943 (Bundesarchiv, unknown)

they were valuable as propaganda to his own people showing that Germany could strike back and exact revenge for the heavy Allied bombing which was wreaking havoc on German cities.

The V2s were developed at the Peenemünde Military Testing site on the island of Usedom off the north German coast. The centre had opened in 1936 as one of Germany's major military research centres under the leadership of Wernher von Braun. A range of rockets and other weaponry was developed there but as early as 1938 work started on what was then known as the A4 rocket – a guided long distance rocket which was in effect the world's first ballistic missile. A production facility was established using forced labour from concentration camps. It is widely believed that more people died in the construction of the V2 than as victims of its deployment.

The first test flight took place in 1942 but an RAF bombing raid known as Operation Hydra on 17 and 18 August 1943 disrupted manufacture plans. Most production moved to an underground facility known as Mittelwerk at Nordhausen in Thuringia. Production continued there and the V2 became an important symbolic, if not military, weapon for Germany until almost the end of the war.

Soviet forces captured the Peenemünde site on 5 May 1945 only to discover that much of it had been destroyed by the retreating Germans.

More interesting, however, to the Western Allies was the technical expertise of the leading German scientists who had been working at Peenemünde; both they and the Soviets were competing for access to the technology that had developed the V2. The Peenemünde director Wernher von Braun and a number of his colleagues had fled the area earlier and surrendered to the Americans. Von Braun played a major role in developing rocket technology in the United States after the war including work on the space programme.

The site itself became a naval base after the war first for the Soviet Union and later for the East German Navy. It was a restricted military area until 1990 and the old ruined power plant was rebuilt by the East Germans and used as a power station.

A museum was opened there in 1992 telling both the Nazi story, including the sufferings of forced labourers, and also the technological narrative. The establishment of the Peenemünde research site back in the 1930s had entirely military motivation but the research undertaken there

Many of the scientists who worked on the development of the V2 at Peenemünde went on to work on the American space programme after the war (Bundesarchiv, unknown)

The Peenemünde site today as a memorial both to technology and to those who suffered and died during the Nazi period (Peter Wippermann)

subsequently did have wider peaceful benefits. Peenemünde can rightly be seen as the birthplace of modern rocket technology. Today more than 150,000 people visit the site annually.

An interesting difference between Peenemünde and other so-called 'perpetrator sites' in Germany is the attitude of local people to this Nazi relic. Talking to staff at many of the sites, there is a distinct feeling that, even now, they would prefer to ignore reminders of the dark past in their own communities. They may accept the idea that it is right for Germany to remember and acknowledge the Nazi past but would prefer it wasn't on their own doorstep. At Peenemünde, however, local pride remains because of its role in revolutionizing technology and it is seen more as an example of brilliant German engineering than as a place of warmongering and suffering. Such is the paradox of Peenemünde.

REICH CHANCELLERY AND FÜHRERBUNKER, BERLIN

The 2004 film Der Untergang (Downfall) vividly portrays the last desperate days of the Nazi regime inside the Führerbunker. Bruno Ganz won plaudits for his rendering of an increasingly erratic and unhinged Hitler although the film was criticised for 'humanising' the Nazi leadership. The movie, however, successfully conveyed the oppressive atmosphere inside the

The entrance to the Führerbunker after Allied bombing – Hitler spent his last few months living underground virtually all the time (Bundesarchiv, unknown)

bunker in the early months of 1945. Hitler's grip on reality loosened as he continued to issue orders to generals who lacked the resources to execute them.

The powerful image still remains of one of the most abhorrent dictators the world has ever seen spending his last days underground pursuing a lost cause and condemning millions more to suffering and death. Contrast this with Churchill's War Rooms – the underground headquarters of the British Prime Minister – from where Britain's wartime leader plotted victory. Both were underground bunkers but so very different both in the popular perception and in their very different outcomes after 1945.

The bunker where the last days of the Third Reich were played out was deep below the garden of the Reich Chancellery in the centre of Berlin. This building was the centrepiece of the German Government although Hitler spent relatively little time in Berlin, particularly during the war. The native Austrian with a fondness for Bavaria was not particularly enamoured of the German capital. Nevertheless, in the death throes of the Nazi regime, he announced that he would stay in his capital city and fight to the last. From January until his suicide at the end of April he spent nearly all his time there.

The original Reich Chancellery had been established as the official residence of the German Chancellor in the Bismarck era in 1878. The building was a revamp of an earlier palace in Wilhelmstrasse. During the Weimar Republic it was extended and, after the Nazis came to power, it was further redeveloped in the mid-1930s as Hitler's residence by the architect

Garden of the Reich Chancellery under which lay the bunker complex where the last days of the Third Reich were played out (Bundesarchiv, unknown)

The new Reich Chancellery, Berlin designed by Albert Speer in the late 1930s (Bundesarchiv, unknown)

Paul Troost. The alterations included the creation in 1936 of an air-raid shelter complex beneath the Chancellery known as the Vorbunker and during the war a deeper bunker, the Führerbunker, was added.

Hitler, however, was dissatisfied with the remodelled Chancellery as the signature building of the Greater German Reich. He asked Albert Speer to create a new, grander building round the corner from the existing Chancellery in Vossstrasse. Buildings were demolished to make way for the new Reich Chancellery which was built by over 4,000 workers on round the clock shifts in less than a year. It was completed in 1938 and Hitler was fulsome in his praise of the building describing Speer as a genius. The new building included a hall of mirrors bigger than that at the Palace of Versailles and, for Hitler and Speer, it was part of the vision of Berlin as the Welthauptstadt or 'World Capital' of a triumphant Greater German Reich.

Inside the Reich Chancellery which was designed to surpass the grand buildings of other great capitals (Bundesarchiv, unknown)

The new Chancellery housed various Reich ministries and was also used as Hitler's military command headquarters when he was in Berlin. Towards the end of the war, with Berlin under aerial bombardment, Hitler retreated into the bunker complex and effectively spent his last four months in the deeper of the two bunkers some 8.5m below the Reich Chancellery garden and protected by several metres of reinforced concrete.

The bunker contained about thirty rooms, including the private quarters of Hitler and Eva Braun, for his senior staff as well as around twenty support staff. It also included the conference room where the increasingly hopeless military situation was reviewed in meetings which regularly went on through the night. The higher Vorbunker was occupied by other senior Nazis including Joseph Goebbels, his wife and six children.

The end is well documented. With Soviet forces fighting their way into the German capital, and nightly Allied air-raids, Berlin was close to collapse. With the Russians only a few hundred metres from the Reich Chancellery Hitler continued issuing wholly unrealistic orders to his generals to counter-attack. He married Eva Braun on 29 April and on the next day, after giving permission for the remaining staff in the bunker to break out, he and Braun committed suicide. Their bodies were burned in the Reich Chancellery Garden. Goebbels whose children were poisoned the following day, then committed suicide with his wife. On 2 May 1945 Soviet troops reached the Führerbunker. The first German surrender document was signed on 7 May.

The post-war treatment of the site of the Führerbunker has been among the most controversial and difficult. Of all the Nazi sites in Germany the place where Hitler met his death might be most likely to be seen as a neo-Nazi shrine. Both the old and new Reich Chancellery buildings were

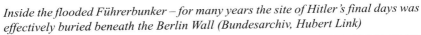

Inside the flooded Führerbunker – for many years the site of Hitler's final days was effectively buried beneath the Berlin Wall (Bundesarchiv, Hubert Link)

Interpretation Board at the site of the Führerbunker – which is deliberately low-key (Colin Philpott)

severely damaged in air raids and artillery bombardment during the last stages of the war. The Soviet occupying forces soon demolished the remaining ruins of the Chancellery buildings but their attempts to blow up the bunkers were only partly successful. Like the Wolfsschanze (The Wolf's Lair) in East Prussia, the structure proved remarkably resilient. Both Soviet and, later, East German attempts to obliterate this most symbolic of Third Reich locations failed.

The problem of what to do with the bunkers disappeared for a generation because the site was very close to the Berlin Wall and part of the undeveloped strip of land nearby. During preparations for the construction of housing on the site in the late 1980s, however, the bunker remains were rediscovered; many of these were destroyed but other parts were simply left and sealed.

In early 2015 'Top Secret', a museum at Duisburg in North-Rhine Westphalia, announced that it was building a replica of the Führerbunker. This attracted widespread criticism inside and outside Germany and was seen by many as an entirely inappropriate 'Disneyfication' of Nazi history.

At the site of the real bunker, however, there is an apartment block and a carpark. A small interpretation board was put up in 2006 at the edge of the carpark to explain the historical significance of the location. The board is deliberately low-key and conveys basic information about the bunker and what happened there.

Visiting this site is the ultimate act of 'dark tourism'. A steady stream of visitors is usually there. The street is named after the Jewish poet and author Gertrud Kolmar who died in Auschwitz. It is in an otherwise anonymous thoroughfare that is unashamedly modern and far removed from the landscape of the 1930s and 1940s. The dark past of this place may have been obliterated but is not forgotten. Together with the interpretation board and its name it is appropriate that the Holocaust Memorial is at the far end of the street.

DRESDEN CITY CENTRE, SAXONY

Curious as it may seem to include the bomb damage in Dresden in an account of sites associated with the Third Reich it remains true that the events of 13-15 February 1945 remain enormously influential in defining both German and British attitudes to the Nazi legacy.

The raid by British and American bombers in the closing months of the war was part of a series of similar raids on German cities which remain controversial seventy years later. A total of more than 1,200 bombers

Dresden City Centre in February 1945 after Allied bombing raids which caused an estimated 25,000 deaths (Bundesarchiv, unknown)

dropped bombs and incendiary devices on the city creating a firestorm which killed an estimated 25,000 people and reduced its historic centre to rubble. Similar raids took place on other German cities in the period and the total number of victims from all such raids has been estimated to be as high as 500,000.

The military justification at the time appears to have centred on the need to support the Russian advance from the east into Germany. The raids would disrupt communications and transport and hamper the ability of the Germans to reinforce the eastern front. Even at the time the raid on Dresden produced some disquiet in Britain and the United States as it was seen as an unnecessary attack on an historic cultural centre – such views were reinforced by the subsequent discovery that many military and industrial targets in Dresden were missed during the raids.

The argument still rages about the rights and wrongs of the bombing. Some historians believe it was a war crime and others that, even if it wasn't a war crime, it was morally indefensible. On the other side is the view that it shortened the war by destroying transport links and damaging morale. Many in Britain also point to the mass bombing of British cities by Germany earlier in the war.

The importance of the Dresden bombing in the context of Nazi architectural legacy is its role in creating a sense of victimhood in Germany after 1945. The country was completely devastated and bankrupt after the war. Much of it lay in ruins and drastic shortages of supplies of food and shelter were exacerbated by streams of expelled refugees flooding from the east. The country was occupied and the moral bankruptcy of the Nazi regime had been laid bare. The process of rooting out those who were 'true' Nazis was underway with evidence being gathered for war crimes trials and for what became known as denazification courts. The only way to deal with this was to try to ignore the horrifying immediate past and regard 1945 as 'Year Zero' or 'Stunde Null' as the Germans described it.

This combination of national shame, physical devastation and the harshness of daily life in impoverished conditions meant that very few Germans had the energy or inclination to manifest a sense of guilt. It was easy for them to see themselves as 'victims' – victims, they believed, of harsh occupiers who, certainly in the case of the Russians, had committed rape on an industrial scale but also victims of unjustified bombing of their cities. Many also saw themselves as victims of the Nazis. These features must form a significant part of the reason why the post-war acknowledgment of Nazi crimes, including the appropriate memorialisation of some of the sites where those crimes were committed, was not a priority. The Dresden bombing was a key event in contributing to that sense of victimhood.

The rebuilt Frauenkirche, Dresden rededicated in 2005 – part of the impressive rebuilding after the wartime damage (Harold Hoyer)

Dresden, like many other German cities, has now been impressively rebuilt. It was part of the Soviet occupation zone and then of East Germany. During that period there was some reconstruction of the city's historic landmarks but more has occurred since reunification – most notably the city's Frauenkirche which was rededicated in 2005. Special services of remembrance still take place in February each year on the anniversary of the raid.

Since 1959 Dresden has been twinned with Coventry, itself the victim of a ferocious German bombing raid in 1940. Significant sums of money were raised in Britain towards the restoration of Dresden's landmarks. Sensitivity over the bombing can, however, still surface. Plans were first made public in 2010 for a plaque in London commemorating the men from Britain's Bomber Command who had died in the Second World War. There was considerable disquiet in Dresden that the victims of the raid carried out by Bomber Command were being ignored and the plaque does now make reference to the victims of the raids. British sensibilities can also be upset; the Archbishop of Canterbury, Justin Welby, was criticized in February 2015 for speaking of his regret over the bombing during the seventieth anniversary service in Dresden.

BERGEN BELSEN CONCENTRATION CAMP, BERGEN, LOWER SAXONY

Dachau was the first permanent concentration camp, Auschwitz the most murderous and Sachsenhausen exemplifies a camp whose terror lived on during the Soviet occupation era. Bergen-Belsen in Lower Saxony is included in this account because of the impact of its liberation on contemporary public opinion.

Bergen-Belsen was not an extermination camp and contained no gas chambers but was, nevertheless, a place of death. An estimated 52,000 people died there between 1940 and 1945 from starvation, disease and maltreatment. Many victims perished in the period immediately around its liberation in April 1945.

Bergen-Belsen had been first established as a prisoner of war camp in 1940. It initially housed Belgian and French POWs but later became a major base for Soviet POWs – an estimated 14,000 of whom died there and in nearby camps.

From 1943 onwards it was taken over by the SS and became a concentration camp. It was used as a holding camp for Jewish prisoners whom the SS hoped to exchange for German POWs held by the Allies. From 1944 it started taking a wider range of prisoners and numbers at the already overcrowded camp grew much larger. When British forces liberated

Bergen-Belsen memorial site today – it was the first in Germany to become an official memorial site (Lower Saxony Memorials Foundation, unknown)

Mass grave at Bergen-Belsen Concentration Camp after its liberation by British troops on 15 April 1945 (UK Government, Sergeant Oaks)

the camp on 15 April 1945, they discovered thousands of unburied corpses and tens of thousands of severely ill prisoners.

The details of the liberation and the press reports and images seen round the world from Bergen-Belsen were some of the most shocking of the twentieth-century. Although other camps in the east like Auschwitz had already been liberated, Bergen-Belsen was perhaps the moment when the full horror of the Holocaust became apparent to the public of the Western Allies. Whatever their governments may have known during the war about the camps, this was the moment when the general public first grasped the scale of the atrocities. The images taken by photographers like Bert Hardy and the graphic accounts of reporters like Richard Dimbleby transmitted the Holocaust into people's homes.

The Germans had agreed to surrender the camp without a fight largely because of an outbreak of typhus. The camp was designed for 10,000 but is estimated to have been holding 60,000 when liberated. Typhus was the main killer and an estimated 500 people a day were dying – a rate which continued for some time after liberation. In the chaotic conditions that followed there were reprisal killings and the Luftwaffe even bombed the camp. Survivors were gradually deloused and moved to a nearby army camp which became a displaced persons camp and remained in use until 1950. Medical teams were brought in from Britain to help deal with the epidemics of disease.

Significant also was the manner of Bergen-Belsen's destruction. In actions repeated at many other liberated concentration camps across Germany, the British forced SS guards to bury the corpses scattered across the camp and local Nazi officials were brought to the camp to witness the horror. The camp was destroyed by British troops, tanks and firebombing not, it would appear, as a symbolic act but as a health measure to halt the typhus epidemic.

After the demolition of the camp the British erected a sign to mark its site and unofficial memorials were placed there to remember the dead of particular countries. The area, however, was ignored until the erection of the first official memorial in 1952 which was initiated by the British occupying authorities and attended by the President of the fledgling West Germany. Bergen-Belsen was the first concentration camp site in Germany itself to become an official memorial site.

As noted previously, however, coming to terms with the Nazi legacy was not a political priority in West Germany until decades later. Bergen-Belsen received attention as the place where one of the Holocaust's best-known victims, Anne Frank, had died. In 1966 the first exhibitions were established on the site but, only after reunification, was it developed further. The memorial site is now the centre of a master plan of

Setting fire to barracks at Bergen-Belsen after the camp's liberation to prevent the spread of disease (UK Government, Bert Hardy)

redevelopment but this will not include the reconstruction of any former buildings. There are walking routes and interactive apps to accompany site tours and over 250,000 people visit Bergen-Belsen annually. It is now supported financially by both the Lower Saxony *Land* Government and the German Federal Government.

SUMMARY

A story which began with the hubris of Nuremberg ends with the moral degradation of Bergen-Belsen. The downfall of any regime is often accompanied by anarchy, chaos and a breakdown of normal moral codes as

Memorial plaque at Bergen-Belsen commemorating the estimated 52,000 people who died there (Arne List)

well as a collapse of basic services. The end of Nazi Germany in 1945 remains, though, a particularly cataclysmic event during which millions of people suffered and died needlessly. It came at the end of a war which could have ended sooner and which had claimed more lives than any other in human history.

Peenemünde, the Führerbunker, Dresden and Bergen-Belsen, each in their own way, epitomise that period of collapse and that sense of the utterly futile, last-ditch nature of the Third Reich's struggle to the bitter end. They also represent the chaos and complete moral collapse by the end of the war. These places also point to the 'Stunde Null' sense which gripped Germany in 1945 and represent defining images which shaped views about the Nazi legacy for generations afterwards.

Conclusion –
Coming to Terms with
the Past
(Vergangenheitsbewältigung)

At the commemoration in January 2015 of the seventieth anniversary of the liberation of the Auschwitz concentration camp, the German President, Joachim Gauck, said 'There is no German identity without Auschwitz… It is part and parcel of our country's history.' Five months earlier Angela Merkel had become the first German Chancellor in office to visit Dachau – the first Nazi concentration camp. She spoke of her 'sadness and shame' and condemned her fellow countrymen who had closed their eyes to the events of the 1930s.

Statements like these by the two most senior figures in the German political establishment demonstrate the level to which acceptance of the country's continuing culpability for what happened under the Third Reich has now become part of Germany's national narrative. As part of this, throughout the country, there are memorials, plaques, documentation centres and other ways of remembering at both 'victim' and 'perpetrator' sites associated with the Nazis.

This is not merely a question of preserving the Third Reich sites and, in many cases, building memorials or museums. Germany has also built completely new structures specifically to commemorate the victims of the Nazis, most notably the Holocaust Memorial in the heart of Berlin or, to give it its correct title, 'The Memorial to the Murdered Jews of Europe'. It was designed by Peter Eisenman and opened in May 2005 – sixty years after the collapse of the Third Reich. The 19,000 square metres site is covered with 2,711 concrete slabs and, underneath it, is an information centre containing the names of all known victims of the Holocaust.

The project was first mooted more than thirty years previously but dogged with delays and controversy. It now stands right at the heart of the German capital very much where the Nazi High Command operated and only a stone's throw from the site of Hitler's bunker.

Walking between the concrete slabs of the memorial laid out on sloping

'Memorial to the Murdered Jews of Europe' – Germany's national memorial to the victims of the Holocaust in the centre of Berlin (ChumChum14)

ground provokes reflection not only about the Holocaust and its attendant horror but also about the current German attitudes it arouses. The memorial represents a remarkable national statement of atonement and remorse. As Neil MacGregor says in his book '*Germany; Memories of a Nation*', 'I know of no other country in the world that, at the heart of its own national capital, erects monuments to its own shame.'

Political apologies for past national misdeeds have become fashionable with Britain apologising for some excesses of its colonial past, France for its treatment of the Jews under the Nazi occupation, and a range of others for their roles in the slave trade. Post-reunification Germany would, nevertheless, appear to be a model for the demonstration of state repentance.

The journey taken, however, by what was, at first, two Germanys has been a long and tortuous one. In essence the fate of the sample of sites covered in this book, and others of which they are representative, fall into three main categories.

The liberation of Bergen-Belsen Concentration Camp in April 1945 – one of many such camps now preserved as memorials (British Army Film Unit, Sergeant Morris)

The first of these are the places most associated with the genocide and the terror of the Nazis – most notably concentration camps but also places like the Gestapo Headquarters in Berlin and the Wannsee House where senior Nazis met to decide on the 'Final Solution'. Of the estimated 15,000 camps established in all countries by the Nazis, many were destroyed either by the Nazis themselves or by the Allies soon after the war. A number were pressed into temporary service as camps by the Allies both for prisoners of war, refugees and alleged Nazi war criminals and, in the case of ten camps in East Germany, as Soviet camps where thousands died in harsh conditions.

Seventy years on, though, a significant number remain as memorials and museums. The original impetus to preserve them as memorials was, in most cases, as a result of 'victim pressure' often in the face of official opposition, particularly in Germany itself. More recently, however, that has changed and now most concentration camp memorials in Germany are supported financially by the Federal Government. In addition, symbolic sites like Wannsee have been preserved and their role in the Third Reich story explained.

The second category is those sites associated with the German war machine – the factories, the U-boat pens, the rocket launch sites and the command bunkers. The fate of these is more mixed. Some are simply war relics no different to those found at military locations in other countries. As elsewhere their future use was determined as much by pragmatic reasons as any other. Some U-boat pens, like the Valentin in Bremen, remain in military use and some factories utilised for the war effort, such as the VW factory in Wolfsburg, remain but have been converted to peaceful ends.

Both at Valentin and Wolfsburg there is now acknowledgement of the suffering that occurred principally through the use of forced labour. Command bunkers mostly have either been left to decay below ground or were destroyed at or shortly after the war's end. The Peenemünde rocket site is preserved as a museum principally for its scientific interest. These military sites seem to have been easier to deal with because they are less strongly associated with the specific crimes and therefore less imbued with the Nazi stigma.

The third main category covers those places specifically built by the Nazis as statements of their power, values and view of the world. These include the Nuremberg Rally Grounds, the buildings on the Obersalzberg near Berchtesgaden, the sites built for the 1936 Olympics, new airports in Berlin and Munich, the party headquarters in various cities and the private homes and grounds acquired or built for the Nazi High Command. A mixture of factors has also been at play in determining the fates of these sites.

The swastika atop the Zeppelin Field grandstand at Nuremberg was symbolically blown up by the Americans. The building and wider site survive partly as a historical relic but also as valuable open space for Nuremberg – the original role of the area before its appropriation. These so-called 'perpetrator sites' like Nuremberg, Berchtesgaden and Munich (which have also opened documentation centres) are perhaps the most interesting in demonstrating how a country can recount the history of its guilt and moral collapse.

Most of the Olympic sites are still in use. Tempelhof and Munich-Riem are no longer airports, not because of any association with the Nazi era, but simply because they were superseded by bigger, more modern airports.

Many Nazi administration buildings have been put to new uses – perhaps most notably the Führerbau where the Munich Agreement was signed in 1938 and which is now a music school. Although most homes of senior Nazis were deliberately demolished by the Allies, or later by the post-war German authorities, some do remain as private residences – including Albert Speer's architectural studio near Berchtesgaden.

The fate of this group of locations demonstrates the perhaps controversial point that architecture is not necessarily bad because it is Nazi architecture. It is difficult to describe the Olympic Stadium in Berlin as an unattractive building and many others were not dissimilar to contemporary buildings created elsewhere. Many British local councils built similarly stark but grand town halls in the 1930s. The post-war conversion of the Nazi holiday camp at Prora-Rügen on the Baltic coast into luxury holiday apartments represents a triumph of pragmatism over symbolism.

More important than what has happened to Nazi buildings is why it has happened. Germany's history of dealing with the physical remains of the Nazi era is, as we have seen, tied to its overall response to the time in question.

For many years only the victims, or their families, and survivors of the Nazi terror (and almost exclusively Jewish victims and survivors), pressed for proper acknowledgement of the significance of places where the Nazis had performed mass murder. For years Germany largely turned a blind eye through a combination of factors. After the war the utter totality of defeat and immediate physical and moral debris meant that dealing with the Nazi legacy simply wasn't important. Survival was the priority and most Germans didn't have the capacity, economically or emotionally, to concern themselves overmuch with the sufferings and injustices which their country had inflicted on millions of others. They saw themselves as victims – victims of ferocious Allied bombing which had reduced their cities to rubble, victims of terrible food shortages, and victims of the forced repatriations from the East.

Later the principal reasons for lack of action were political pragmatism, guilt and complicity. The generation in power in post-war Germany included many people who were implicated to a greater or lesser extent in the Nazi story particularly after the process of denazification slowed down. The Western Allies occupying Germany in the late 1940s largely lost interest in pursuing Nazi perpetrators as the priority was building up what became West Germany as a bulwark against communism and the Soviet Union.

As Germans themselves regained control of their government many had been part of the Nazi regime and had no interest in raking over its era. Germany would almost certainly have been ungovernable had everyone with any level of Nazi complicity been excluded from public or political office.

As a younger post-war generation challenged their parents in the 1960s and beyond the Nazi era was opened up to greater examination and a process began of dealing with the period including the physical legacy of buildings and places. The continued division of Germany remained an obstacle because the Nazi legacy became a political football for the two states. East Germany portrayed the West as the successor fascist state to the Third Reich, and the West was more focussed on the evils of a communist dictatorship on its doorstep than one that had disappeared more than twenty years earlier. Important also were differences within West Germany. which persisted after the fall of the Berlin Wall, between cities which felt more or less comfortable with their Nazi past – with Munich notably slower than elsewhere to acknowledge its role as the 'capital of the movement'.

It was only after German reunification in 1990 that the process of 'Vergangenheitsbewältigung' or coming to terms with the past gained real momentum. The generation that was most complicit in the Nazi story had mainly died and there was an increasing willingness to tackle the difficulties of the era as the reunited country became politically and economically powerful again and imbued with growing self-confidence. Hence there followed the Holocaust Memorial in Berlin, the development of documentation centres and other memorials and museums at both 'victim' and 'perpetrator' sites and a much more open and frank discussion about the Nazi legacy.

An alternative interpretation is that the memorials and documentation centres suggest something other than a country which has come to terms with its complicity in one of the worst regimes in history. This strand of opinion sees documentation centres in Nuremberg, Berlin, Munich and elsewhere (and 'Third Reich Tours') as pandering to a questionable fascination with so-called 'dark places' and suggests that benefits from exploiting any such tourism trade are morally dubious. They also consider the expense of 70 million Euros to save the Nuremberg Rally Grounds from collapse to be complete anathema. There is, furthermore, a lingering concern that overemphasizing Nazi sites, particularly the so-called 'perpetrator sites', could have a dangerous potential to encourage neo-Nazis.

A further issue is increasingly raised by those who question why there is so much continuing interest in the Nazi period and its associated crimes relative to the interest in documenting and dealing with the crimes committed under of the Communist dictatorship which governed part of German territory for over forty years after 1945. Such criticism points to the crimes, particularly in Eastern Europe, under Soviet rule. The seventieth anniversary of the bombing of Dresden in February 2015 also highlighted

Inside the half-built Congress Hall at the Nuremberg Rally Grounds site – (Magnus Gerdkemper)

once again the continuing doubts about the legitimacy of Allied bombing of German cities towards the end of the war. These and other examples raise the question of moral relativism about the behaviour of different regimes and different countries.

There is, of course, no simple right or wrong view. My own experience of visiting many Nazi sites in Germany leaves me in no doubt that, overall, Germany is a country handling its difficult past seriously and with a degree of critical reflection that is admirable. Germany has agonised over its Nazi legacy. The memorial sites are solemn and chilling and no-one who visits Dachau or Auschwitz can fail to be impressed by the simple commemoration of multiple victims that these places now offer. Professor John Lennon, who created the term 'dark tourism', believes that Germany has dealt with the physical legacy of Nazism relatively well compared with many other countries who have been less transparent about dark periods in their histories. He highlights the emphasis on documentation and evidence-based interpretation in written and visual form and believes that this approach has evolved after deep consideration and reflection.

Visiting the documentation centres in Nuremberg, Berchtesgaden, Berlin and elsewhere, did not leave me feeling that there was an attempt to explain away and exculpate. There may well have been a mixture of motives in the decisions that led to the opening of these centres. My overall opinion, however, is that they are an honest attempt to describe places of significance in German history to people within and beyond Germany.

The Nazis did not have a monopoly of terror and human history is sadly littered with repugnant regimes. It will remain vital, however, that the story of how Germany became the Third Reich, and the ensuing catastrophe, is told for future generations. The history of the buildings and spaces where that story unfolded is a crucial element in ensuring that the tragedy is understood and never repeated.

Sources and Bibliography

BOOKS

Beyond Berlin – Twelve German Cities Confront the Nazi Past; Gavriel D. Rosenfeld, Paul B. Jaskot, University of Michigan Press 2008

Dark Tourism; The Attraction of Death and Disaster; John Lennon and Malcolm Foley, Cengage Learning EMA, 2010

Haunted City, Nuremberg and the Nazi Past, Neil Gregor, Yale University Press, 2008

The Nuremberg Rallies, Alan Wykes, Macdonald and Co, 1969

Germany, Memories of a Nation, Neil MacGregor, Allen Lane, 2014

Hitler's Olympics, Christopher Hilton, Sutton Publishing, 2006

The Good Nazi; the Life and Lies of Albert Speer, Dan van der Vat, Weidenfeld and Nicolson, 1997

Exorcising Hitler, the Occupation and Denazification of Germany, Frederick Taylor, Bloomsbury, 2011

Germania, Simon Winder, Picador, 2010

Coping with the Nazi Past; West German debates on Nazism and Generational Conflict, 1955-1975, Philipp Gassert and Alan E. Steinweis, Berghahn Books, 2006.

That Was Dachau, 1933-1945, Stanislav Zamecnik, Le Cherche Midi, 2004

The End, Germany 1944-45, Ian Kershaw, Allen Lane 2011.

The Nazis' Nuremberg Rallies, James Wilson, Pen and Sword, 2012

Germany 1945 – From War to Peace; Richard Bessel, Simon and Schuster, 2009

A Social History of the Third Reich, Richard Grunberger, Weidenfeld and Nicolson, 1971

West Germany and the Nazi legacy, Caroline Sharples, Routledge Studies in Modern European History, 2012

The Obersalzberg and the Third Reich, Verlag Anton Plenk, 2008

After the Battle Edition 19; the Führerhauptquartiere; Edited by Winston G.Ramsey, Battle of Britain International Ltd, 1977.

Art under Fascism, Roberta Pergher, 2007

ARTICLES

The Myth of Hitler's Role in Building the Autobahn; Deutsche Welle article by W.Dick & A.Lichtenberg (2012)

Deutsche Welle article on the filming of 'Valkyrie' 2008

'If you could see the place now, Adolf' article by William Cook, the Guardian, 2002

Allan Hall article on Berlin Olympic Village, Daily Mail, 2014

'A Visit to Hermann Göring's Carinhall' by Josephine Cowdery, 2007.

Lucy Crossley article on theft of 'Arbeit macht frei' sign from Dachau; Daily Mail, 2014

David Crossland article on Spiegel Online about Bomber Command plaque, 2010.

Jess Smee article on Hamburg flaktower becoming a biomass plant; Spiegel Online 2011

Christoph Gunkel; Forbidden Pictures in Hitler's Bunker, Der Spiegel, 2013

Anthony Beevor article on plans to recreate the Führerbunker, Daily Telegraph, 2015

Andreas Meyhof & Gerhard Pfeil, Garmisch-Partenkirchen's Uncomfortable Past; Der Spiegel, 2010

War History Online article on Germania plans, 2014

Joe Carroll; Berlin Lays its History Bare; Irish Times article, 2014

Sabine Brantl, Haus der Kunst, München. Ein Ort und seine Geschichte im Nationalsozialismus, Munich, 2007

Lucy Burns article on 'Why Hitler hated modernism' BBC News website, 2013.

Symbols and Silences of National Memory – Commemorations of the Nazi Era in Berlin; Paper by Professor Harold Marcuse

Tony Paterson article on plans for Nuremberg Rally Grounds, the Independent, 2013

'Complex Riese' Paper by Krzyzowa Foundation for Mutual Understanding in Europe and the Mittelbau-Dora Concentration Camp Memorial

Triana Moore article 'Holiday Camp with a Nazi Past' for BBC News website, 2008

Anthony Fiola, Washington Post article on Prora-Rügen, 2014

Ella Morton article on Prora-Rügen, Atlas Obscura, 2014

Eva Munk article on Schindler factory, Times of Israel, 2012

Ladka Bauerova article for Bloomberg News on Schindler factory, 2014

Raul Colon; Nazi Germany's European U-boat bases and pens after the war on military discussion forum

David Crossland article on Wewelsburg Castle in Der Spiegel, 2010

Wirtschaftswoche article on German company collaboration with Nazis, 2014

Sara Malm article on Wolf's Lair, Daily Mail 2012

Art and Architecture towards political crises; the 1937 Paris International Exposition in Context; article in CultureAllroundMan, 2014

Katja Sebald article on Deutsches Stadion plan in Der Spiegel, 2012

Desmond Butler article in the New York Times on Sachsenhausen Camp during Soviet era, 2001.

WEBSITES

http://www.gdw-berlin.de
www.stiftung-bg.de
www.bergen-belsen.stiftung-ng.de
http://museums.nuremberg.de/documentation-centre/
www.olympiastadion-berlin.de
www.strecke46.de
http://www.kz-gedenkstaette-dachau.de/
http://www.kz-gedenkstaette-leonberg.de/
http://berliner-unterwelten.de/home.1.1.html
http://www.obersalzberg.de/obersalzberg
http://www.hausderkunst.de/
http://www.yadvashem.org/yv/en/museum/
http://www.topographie.de/
http://www.hofbraeuhaus.de/
http://www.ns-dokumentationszentrum-muenchen.de/centre
http://www.vogelsang-ip.de
http://www.ordensburg.info/
http://www.peenemuende.de/
www.dokumentationszentrum-prora.de
www.thirdreichruins.com
www.bundestag.de
www.tannenberg-denkmal.de
www.mhk.pl
www.thf-berlin.de
www.munich-airport.de
www.denkort-bunker-valentin.de
www.ghwk.de
http://www.wewelsburg.de/en/
http://www.stiftung-bg.de/gums/en/
http://auschwitz.org/en/
http://www.stiftung-denkmal.de/

Acknowledgements

I would like to thank the many people who have helped with the writing and publication of this book.

They include staff at documentation centres, memorial sites and museums across Germany and beyond for their invaluable help with particular thanks to Marco Esseling, Dirk Riedel, Florian Dierl, Chris Jasch, Alex Drecoll, Jens-Christian Wagner, Phillip Aumann, Dieter Stockmann, Sabine Brantl, Christoph Schuster and Ulla Britte.

Also to colleagues in the UK who have helped with its production and promotion including John Lennon, Neil Gregor, Geoff Walden, William Cook, Neil MacGregor, Martin Stephens, Sitesh Patel, Paul Richards, Paul Goodman, Tim Padfield, Syima Aslam, Irna Qureshi, Nick Baines, Sarah Mitchell, Joan Concannon; and staff at the British Library and the JB Priestley Library at the University of Bradford.

To the team at Pen and Sword Books including Henry Wilson, Matt Jones, Jon Wilkinson, Katie Eaton, Kate Bamforth and Chris Robinson.

All images used in this book have been credited where possible in the captions. We have made our best efforts to do this accurately from information available and have contacted rights holders where appropriate and possible.

Finally, special thanks to Dave Gardner, Alex Philpott and Hilary Philpott for their help with translation, proof reading and advice.

Index